THE STRENGTH OF A GOOD SOLDIER OF JESUS CHRIST
APPEARS IN NOTHING MORE THAN IN STEADFASTLY
MAINTAINING THE HOLY CALM, MEEKNESS,
SWEETNESS AND BENEVOLENCE
OF HIS MIND, AMIDST ALL THE STORMS,
INJURIES, STRANGE BEHAVIOR AND SURPRISING ACTS
AND EVENTS OF THIS EVIL
AND UNREASONABLE WORLD.

(JONATHAN EDWARDS)

A LIFEGUIDE® RESOURCE

DRAWING CLOSE TO GOD

The Essentials of a Dynamic Quiet Time

Stephen D. Eyre

InterVarsity Press
Downers Grove, Illinois

InterVarsity Press® is the book-publishing division of InterVarsity Christian Fellowship®, a student movement active on campus at hundreds of universities, colleges and schools of nursing in the United States of America, and a member movement of the International Fellowship of Evangelical Students. For information about local and regional activities, write Public Relations Dept., InterVarsity Christian Fellowship, 6400 Schroeder Rd., P.O. Box 7895, Madison, WI 53707-7895.

All Scripture quotations, unless otherwise indicated, are taken from the HOLY BIBLE, NEW INTERNATIONAL VERSION®. NIV®. Copyright © 1973, 1978, 1984 by International Bible Society. Used by permission of Zondervan Publishing House. All rights reserved.

Chapter 8 is adapted from Quiet Time Dynamics, by Stephen Eyre, InterVarsity Press, 1989.

Cover photograph: J. C. Leacock
ISBN 0-8308-1184-2

Printed in the United States of America ∞

Library of Congress Cataloging-in-Publication Data

Eyre, Stephen D., 1948-
    Drawing close to God: the essentials of a dynamic quiet time:
   with guided quiet times/Stephen D. Eyre.
      p.   cm.
    Includes bibliographical references.
    ISBN 0-8308-1184-2 (paper: alk. paper)
    1. Spiritual life—Christianity.   2. Devotional exercises.
  I. Title.
  BV4501.2.E95   1995
  248.4'6—dc20   95-40449
                                        CIP

17	16	15	14	13	12	11	10	9	8	7	6	5	4	3	2	1
09	08	07	06	05	04	03	02	01	00	99	98	97	96	95

To Jacalyn
It's words, words, words.

1

The Benefits
of a
Quiet Time

W_here is God?"_

My faith seemed like a burden, and the uncertain future appeared to be a dead end. And God was silent. Or if he was speaking and guiding, it was not apparent to me.

We were living in England on a short-term mission assignment. Our term was almost over, the lease on our house was about to expire, and my current ministry contract was coming to an end. Things did not look good for a new position on the other side of the Atlantic. I felt the weight of providing for my family. I knew I was supposed to trust God, but struggled with a sense of panic.

At one point I sensed a burning urge rising within me that seemed to say, _You aren't doing what you know._ Whether that "urge" came from God or my own insight I don't know. But it was right on target.

I had practiced quiet times for years, but in the crises of the past months they had become occasional and haphazard. So I renewed my commitment and set aside time in my schedule. No immediate deliverance came, although eventually God opened doors for me. What did happen was that I became able to believe that the God who brought me across the Atlantic could get me back. God was there after all.

I need quiet times because I need God. He is the one who makes sense of life for me, in times of crisis or calm. J. I. Packer writes, "The world becomes a strange, mad, painful place and life in it a disappointing and unpleasant business, for those who do not know God. Disregard the study of God and you sentence yourself to stumble through life blindfolded, as it were, with no sense of direction and no understanding of what surrounds you. This way you can waste your life and lose your soul."[1]

In my quiet time I find the knowledge of God that makes sense of life. A quiet time is like a looking glass, a sort of magic mirror, that lets me look into the deeper dimensions of life. Through the mirror I am able to see the reality of God's presence. I can look not only at God but also at myself. Without that mirror God seems distant, and I tend to lose my Christian perspective on the world around me.

I need the mirror of a quiet time to be a normal Christian. It's like the mirror in the bathroom. I suppose I could shave without it, but a few whiskers here and there would be left uncut, and numerous razor nicks would appear. I also need the mirror on the dresser to make sure that my shirt is tucked in right and that my tie (when I wear one) is straight.

I need the mirror of a quiet time to show me that God is really present in my life. As a Christian I *believe* that he is. But my *experience* of spiritual reality tends to vary. Like most Americans, I have been conditioned to believe that my personal value depends on my productivity.

Who has time to think about God when there is so much to do? As I look at my life in the mirror of my quiet time, I feel God's presence. I continue to be busy but feel less driven.

I also need the mirror to look into the depths of my soul. The lintel above the ancient Greek oracle in Delphi bore the words "Know Thyself." A quiet time helps me do that. When I practice the discipline of a quiet time, I am able to look beneath my own surface. Who am I? What forces have shaped me? What needs, desires and fears direct me? Is God really at work within?

But looking in the mirror can also be threatening and uncomfortable. I have experienced quiet times when buried thoughts, motivations and unwanted emotions suddenly rose up. This scared me so much once that I stopped having quiet times for a while. Finally I picked up the mirror again because looking in it was the only way to get to the other side of my fears. In the presence of God the deep pains that surfaced were changed, cleansed and transformed. Most of all, I grew in the knowledge of God. Like Job I was able to say what I couldn't have said before: "My ears had heard of you but now my eyes have seen you" (Job 42:5).

Discovering Quiet Times

I have not always been an advocate of quiet times. In the early years of my Christian life, I read the Bible like a novel or a textbook. I didn't read religiously or on a schedule; I just read. I prayed for things as I needed them, when I needed them. More often than not, I was delightfully surprised when my prayers were answered.

I first encountered the idea of a daily quiet time at a weekend conference during graduate school. I wasn't impressed. I felt it was for religious people who were into rituals and traditions. Over the next several years, however, I had a change of heart. I came to realize that just as my body needs regular meals to be healthy and energetic, so my relationship with God also needs regular nourishment. When I began to have a regular quiet time, I didn't experience any fireworks. But I felt good, as I did after running a couple of miles. I knew that my quiet time would bring me spiritual knowledge, strength and endurance if I kept it up.

Getting Started

Sharing a quiet time with someone else is the best way to get started. For a number of years, I have met with diverse groups of people, explaining how to have a quiet time. After we have gone through the spiritual exercises, we talk about the experience. Again and again I am delighted to discover that God is at work in me and my friends. I have coined the phrase "guided quiet times" to describe these meetings.

I wish that I could meet with you so that we could have a couple of guided times together. Since the chances of that are slim, I have included a guided quiet time at the end of each chapter. These quiet times are adapted from my series, Spiritual Encounter Guides. At the end of each quiet time I've noted which guide it is taken from. Each one includes an introduction that welcomes you into your time with God and sets a passage of Scripture into its context. Then step by step I lead you through Bible study, reflection questions and prayer.

All that you need for each quiet time is a Bible, writing materials (pen and notebook) and a desire to meet God. It is possible to go through the quiet times in five or six minutes while you briskly fill in the blanks. If you do that, I doubt that you will get much out of them. However, if you ponder the questions and prayerfully write out your responses, spending twenty minutes or more, I suspect that you will be delightfully surprised at what happens.

Guided Quiet Time
God for You (Colossians 1:15-20)

Thinking about God is important. A. W. Tozer wrote, "What comes into your mind when you think about God is the most important thing about you."

Thinking about God is important, but it is not easy. Our impressions of other people are usually based on their physical appearance. Writers create mental images for us by describing a person's appearance and behavior. But how do we describe someone who is invisible?

Our mental images of God come from a variety of sources—our parents, ministers or close friends who talk about God. Hollywood and the media communicate a contemporary image of God that varies from nonexistent to some vague impersonal force that we can learn to manipulate.

How can the human mind ever conceive of the infinite, eternal God? J. B. Phillips wrote a book about this with a great title, *Your God Is Too Small.* He feels that our images of God are too small and defective. Consider what the apostle Paul tells us about Jesus Christ: "He is the *image* of the invisible God."

Approach

What do you think God is like? Write down a description of the images that come to mind. Ask God to help you sort the images that are healthy from the ones that may be unhealthy.

Study

1. Read Colossians 1:15-20. Paul uses a number of striking words and phrases to describe Jesus. He is the firstborn over all creation. Describe the extent of Jesus' authority and power.

2. Jesus is also the firstborn over the church. What does Paul mean by this?

3. In verse 19 the apostle writes of the "fullness of God" dwelling in Jesus. False teachers used this term to refer to the "secret essence of the universe." In contrast, what is Paul teaching about Jesus and his reconciling work?

Reflect

1. These descriptions of Jesus show what God is really like. How does this make you feel about God?

2. As I finished my quiet time for this day, I came up with these identifications of Jesus:

Visible God; Creator God; Personal God; Human God; Pain-Filled God; Peaceful God.

Spend some time in prayer reflecting on Jesus as the Lord of all creation. Perhaps you could imagine him in heaven on a throne surrounded by divine beings who are in submission to him. Write down what you feel as you consider his glory.

3. Consider Jesus rising from the tomb on Easter morning. Perhaps you could see behind him the numberless others who will be raised from the dead. Consider yourself also as one of those who have been resurrected. Write what you feel as you consider the resurrection life he provides for you.

Pray

Choose one of the descriptions of Jesus listed above or think of your own, and respond with praise and thanksgiving for who he is and what he has done. Take your concerns and needs to him as well, knowing that he wants to respond to you.

[Taken from day 5 of *Sinking Your Roots in Christ*, by Stephen D. Eyre, InterVarsity Press, 1992.]

2

Why You Need
a Quiet Time

Several years ago I visited the Art Institute of Chicago. I took an entire day to walk through the European art, beginning in the fourteenth century and moving from room to room until I reached the twentieth century. The early rooms contained nothing but religious art; the last rooms, nothing but secular art. Somewhere along the way subjects other than God became more interesting to Western artists.

As the morning wore on, the images began to run together. I left the Art Institute, went down the steps past the lions, crossed Michigan Avenue, dodged several cars and went to lunch a couple of blocks away. After lunch I resumed my pilgrimage. The seventeenth and eighteenth centuries were my favorites. Technique was vastly improved, and not all the art was religious. I actually found that a relief. God is revealed in all of life.

Finally I came to twentieth-century and modern art: incoherent forms in unrecognizable scenes. The works seemed harsh and metallic. I felt more affinity with the early European paintings. It was easy to think about God in rooms filled with Christian art and religious symbols. It felt "normal."

I felt no affinity with the works of my age. In the twentieth-century rooms I felt "abnormal." There was no place for God. Not that he was openly denied or attacked—he just wasn't there. In those rooms I felt out of place, uncomfortable, even lonely. My faith didn't fit. I felt immersed in spiritual blindness and the absence of God.

Modern culture affects me the same way. God has been intellectually, socially and institutionally excluded from the college campus, the marketplace and leisure time. We are socialized into unbelief and spiritual darkness. It is as if we are standing on an escalator that is constantly moving downward. Educated into a one-dimensional reality, it is hard for us to believe in the existence of anything beyond the five senses. Heaven, hell, God, the soul, prayer—these things aren't tangible, so we doubt that they are real, even if we are determined to believe they are.

Most Western Christians have been influenced by secular culture. Like everyone else, we go through the day with little occasion to call on God. Unless we take conscious precautions, we too can develop God-blindness. A colorblind person can't see red or green because the rods and cones in the eye are damaged. Many colorblind people are unaware of their condition until they reach their teens. They use the words *red* and *green* without having any experience of the actual colors.

God-blindness works the same way. The rods and cones of our spiritual eyes are damaged. We have the word *God* in our vocabulary, but the experience of God is missing. And like colorblind people, we go about our lives without realizing that something is wrong. When we practice quiet time, we counter the forces of God-blindness. Quiet time focuses our spiritual sight so that we can meet with God.

Avoiding God

According to Genesis 3, God met Adam and Eve each afternoon for a walk. But then they sinned and hid themselves in the bushes. Ever since, human beings have moved farther and farther away from God. This avoidance of God is our spiritual disease. We are all in the bushes because God makes us uncomfortable.

This allergic reaction to God is not limited to the ungodly. The history of Israel is a record of repeated running away from God. Even King David, a man after God's own heart, wrote in one of his psalms, "Where can I flee from your presence?" (Ps 139:7).

I don't have to look very deep to find this dynamic of avoidance active in my own heart. In my early teenage years I didn't want anything to do with God. I left the church and God when I was fourteen and began to look for meaning in other directions. It was the sixties, the Age of Aquarius, the era of universal peace and love. It was the era of the Beatles, the Rolling Stones and Crosby, Stills, Nash and Young. I grew my hair and played guitar. In the midst of this cultural ferment, my father married a woman who was outspoken about her faith in God. During the first year of their marriage, I avoided her as much as I could. I left the house early and came home late.

One evening two young men from my stepmother's church showed up at my front door and asked if they could come in for a chat. I allowed them to come in but told them they were wasting their time. Sitting down on the couch, they asked a few casual questions and then began to talk about God. Cutting them off, I informed them that I had given up my faith in God. I was sure that Christianity was irrelevant and scientifically disproved. They listened and didn't say much. I told them that I knew my life was empty and I was in need of something. But God, the God of Christianity, was going to be the last direction I investigated.

Not long after their visit, my resistance to God began to crumble. My car needed repair work, so my stepmother gave me a ride to work every morning. For a week I endured the raspy voice and haranguing message of a radio preacher that she listened to on the way into town. Most days I lay on the back seat, exhausted and hung over from the previous night's "fun." Yet through the haze, that raspy voice had a ring of truth. It was as if somehow that old preacher knew me. Through his words, in some strange way, I was personally addressed. I found myself wanting to believe.

It is a good thing for me that God is not put off by resistance. He continues to seek us even as we run.

I can even turn my own spiritual pursuits into a substitute for God. I remember spending a good part of one morning in serious study of the Scriptures. Suddenly I had a strong sense that God was sitting in a chair beside the desk. I felt a pull on my heart to put down my pen, turn to face him and just sit in quiet heartfelt worship. My response to this sense of call was irritation. I had determined that this was to be a study time. I wanted to wave away this call, grumbling, "Not now, God; can't you see I'm studying the Bible?"

Attending church and all sorts of religious activities can have the appearance of seeking God when in fact it is another means of avoidance. Rousing worship services full of inspiring music and moving prayers are not enough to overcome this. Nor is being doctrinally correct a guarantee that we are OK. In fact, all of these can be dangerous, because they allow us to cherish the illusion that we are spiritually growing when in fact we are in spiritual darkness. Isaiah wrote about outward forms of religious practice, "These people . . . honor me with their lips, but their hearts are far from me" (Is 29:13).

One of the seven deadly sins that Christians in the Middle Ages feared was sloth. Thomas Aquinas defined sloth as "sorrow about spiritual good." It is a joylessness about God, who is the source of all joy. It is despairing passiveness that gives up on seeking God. It is a cold sin that has passed beyond disobedience and rebellion. Sloth is what happens to us when we avoid God and then pretend that we are still religious.

The compulsive busyness of our culture is also a means of avoiding God. Most of us spend forty to sixty hours a week at work. We spend another ten to twenty hours in front of the television. Details of living like paying bills, keeping up the house and chauffeuring children eat up the rest of the week. Even as we maintain such a crazy pace, we lament it. Why do we drive ourselves? It's just another way to avoid a divine encounter. If we ever slowed down, the presence of God might just begin to get through.

Slowing down and getting quiet then is just what we must do. As we practice quiet time, we begin to counter spiritual apathy. As our churches encourage us to move beyond being busy with Christian activities and understand the faith as more than Sunday worship, they will become powerhouses for God. God is there to meet us if we open up.

Guided Quiet Time
Resisting God

> Where can I go from your Spirit? Where can I flee from your presence? (Ps 139:7)

While there is something deep within us that longs for God, we sometimes avoid him as well. During a counseling session, a young woman came face to face with her avoidance:

> "I'm not sure what I am upset about, but I know it has to do with the way I see God," she said. "I realized that I keep God at a distance. I want to know him, but I don't. It's like Jesus is standing at the door of my life and I have it open just a crack. If I open it all the way, I am sure that he is going to burst in and tell me I have to be a nun. I hope that if I can just keep his laws and don't look at him directly, then maybe I can still live my life the way I want to."[1]

There are various reasons for avoiding God:

> We feel guilty and are afraid to face him.

We are disappointed by him.

We are angry at him and feel that he has let us down.

We are afraid that he will make unreasonable demands on us.

If we are to grow spiritually, we must be able to discern how we avoid God. One of my personal patterns of avoidance is the "just a minute" syndrome. When I sit down to read Scripture, my eye will catch a magazine article that I want to read. I put down my Bible, telling myself I'll get back to the Scriptures in just a couple of minutes. But somehow I never do. Another of my patterns is the "I'm too busy" syndrome. Initially, my excuse is that there is too much to do today, and I'll get to it tomorrow. But "tomorrow" turns out to be a couple of weeks.

Approach

Make a list of things that come between you and him. Lift each one up to the Lord and ask him to take it.

Study

1. Let's look at this principle of avoidance. Read Genesis 3:6-10. What's going on?

2. Read Psalm 53:2-3. Summarize its meaning.

3. Jesus confronted religious leaders who appeared to be seeking God but in fact were not. In Mark 7:6 he says: "Isaiah was right when he prophesied about you hypocrites; as it is written: 'These people honor me with their lips, but their hearts are far from me.' " What is Jesus' point?

Reflect

1. If we are to grow spiritually, we must be able to identify and eliminate the ways in which we avoid God. What patterns of ingrained avoidance do you see in your own life?

2. What difference would it make in your life if you stopped avoiding him?

Pray
Ask God to help you identify patterns of avoidance. Ask him to free you from these patterns so that you can grow in seeking him.

[Taken from day 2 of *Entering God's Presence*, by Stephen D. Eyre, InterVarsity Press, 1992.]

3

What Is
a Quiet Time?

A *quiet time is a meeting with God. The presence of God is the* birthright of every believer. This is important to fix in your mind. Otherwise quiet time can become merely a set of routines and techniques for Bible study and prayer. As we cultivate a quiet time, we take seriously the pervasive theme of Christianity, that the presence of God is our birthright. The angel named Jesus Immanuel, which means "God with us." Jesus' last words recorded by Matthew are "Surely I am with you always, to the very end of the age" (Mt 28:20).

God's abiding presence is a special blessing offered to Israelite leaders in the Old Testament. Abraham, Joshua, Samuel, David and Jeremiah were among those who knew and expected the presence of God. Moses' expectation of the presence of God is especially inspiring to me. After his encounter at the burning bush, the presence of God became the norm of his life, and he was not willing to live without it.

After the golden calf incident Moses lamented the burden of leadership and asked for guidance. The Lord responded, "My Presence will go with you, and I will give you rest." To this Moses replied, "If your Presence does not go with us, do not send us up from here. How will anyone know that you are pleased with me and with your people unless you go with us? What else will distinguish me and your people from all the other people on the face of the earth?" (Ex 33:14-16).

As he led the nation, Moses set up a tent called the "tent of meeting" on the outskirts of the Israelite camp. There people could "inquire of the Lord." In that tent Moses met with God "face to face." When we have a quiet time, we are setting up a tent of meeting, a place outside the busy routines of our lives where we can be with God.

The Pursuit of God

Meeting with God is never easy. The author of Hebrews writes that "anyone who comes to him must believe that he exists and that he rewards those who earnestly seek him" (Heb 11:6). Through the prophet Jeremiah, God says to Judah, "You will seek me and find me when you seek me with all your heart" (Jer 29:13). We must reach out for God even as we sit down to be with him.

A. W. Tozer observed that "contemporary Christians have been caught in the spurious logic that those who have found him need no longer seek him." Nothing could be farther from the truth. The paradox of the Christian faith is that those who know him are those who seek him. Tozer writes, "Come near to the holy men and women of the past and you will soon feel the heat of their desire after God. They mourned for Him, they prayed and wrestled and sought for Him day and night, in season and out, and when they found Him, the finding was all the sweeter for the long seeking."[1]

The psalms provide interior glimpses of those who knew and pursued

God. David writes, "One thing I ask of the LORD, this is what I seek: that I may dwell in the house of the LORD all the days of my life, to gaze upon the beauty of the LORD and to seek him in his temple" (Ps 27:4). In another psalm he says, "My soul thirsts for God, for the living God. When can I go and meet with God?" (Ps 42:2). In Psalm 84 we read, "My soul yearns, even faints, for the courts of the LORD; my heart and my flesh cry out for the living God" (Ps 84:2). These psalms stir up our hearts to pursue God as well as record the psalmist's pursuit of him.

The language of Christian spirituality is filled with words like desire, thirst, hunger, pining, seeking, restlessness and yearning. Bernard of Clairvaux (1090-1153) wrote, "We taste of Thee, O Thou Living Bread, And long to feast upon Thee still; We drink of Thee, the Fountainhead And Thirst our souls from Thee to fill." Jonathan Edwards, the leader of the first Great Awakening in the American colonies in the eighteenth century, wrote, "Spiritual good is of a satisfying nature. . . . And the more a man experiences this . . . satisfying sweetness, the more earnestly will he hunger and thirst for more."[2]

During a quiet time we can experience that satisfying sweetness to which Edwards and St. Bernard refer. We create the time and space for God's Spirit to break through. Occasionally something rises up—a yearning toward God. I never know exactly why it happens, but there is a sense of being drawn. Like embers that become a crackling fire when they are fanned, a yearning for God fills my heart and cries out, "Abba, Father" (Gal 4:6). I know cognitively *and* affectively that I belong to God. Affection and gratitude brim over in my heart. When that happens, I usually close my Bible, put away my prayer lists and just sit in worship.

It is always possible to know God better than we do. Paul prays for the Ephesian church that God "may give you the Spirit of wisdom and revelation, so that you may know him better" (Eph 1:17). We need to press on. Having a quiet time is an essential way to do that.

The Practice of Spiritual Disciplines

Even as I encounter God and pursue him, knowledge of him can elude me. I become frustrated with the disparity between my knowledge, actions and thought patterns. Doctrinal formulations alone do not keep me in healthy fellowship with God, as Jesus' encounters with the Pharisees and Sadducees illustrate. Nor are shaking experiences with the Holy Spirit (I have had a few of them) enough to sustain me in daily holiness.

In my four years at seminary I read a lot about God. But reading a profound truth in Scripture or a great Christian book did not cause me to appropriate it into the daily patterns of my life. I needed to encounter God's truth in a transforming way. As I struggled with this, I discovered spiritual disciplines, such as solitude, silence, fasting and meditation. While not means of achieving salvation, these disciplines do promote spiritual growth in Jesus Christ.

The term "spiritual disciplines" may conjure up images of hooded monks chanting in the early hours of the morning. These monks have left the world in order to pursue an ascetic lifestyle—most impractical for us "normal" folk. In reality, spiritual disciplines are tremendously practical. They are truly essential to those who experience the daily challenge of living out their Christian lives in the marketplace.

Throughout this book, I am going to focus on several disciplines which fit into a half-hour quiet time. *Silence* is the discipline of getting quiet so you can listen for the Lord. *Solitude* is the discipline of setting aside some place where you and the Lord can be alone together. *Bible study* is the discipline that helps you grasp the meaning of the biblical text. *Meditation* is the discipline that helps you penetrate and embrace the Scriptures. *Prayer* is the discipline of asking God for help for yourself and others. While I won't specifically address worship or confession, these disciplines will begin to show up naturally (supernaturally) as the Lord meets you.

As I began to practice spiritual disciplines in my quiet time, my spiritual senses developed. I spent time in meditation, looking to God with the eyes of my heart. Although I didn't see him in a physical sense, I perceived his presence and knew he was there. As I stopped doing all the talking in prayer and began to listen with spiritual ears, answers came to questions that I had been struggling with. And more than just answers, a restful, even tender quiet filled me. I knew that God loved me and that he is good.

Spiritual Desire

The human heart has an innate hunger for God. Psychoanalyst Gerald May writes in his book *Addiction and Grace,* "After twenty years of listening to the yearnings of people's hearts, I am convinced that all human beings have an inborn desire for God. Whether we are consciously religious or not, this desire is our deepest longing and our most precious treasure."[3] Quiet times allow us to properly address that hunger.

Just as we can't live without daily bread, we can't live without daily feeding on the life of our Creator and Savior. God's Spirit inside believers creates a taste for him. Through his work inside our hearts, we come to relish his Word. It becomes "sweeter than honey" (Ps 19:10). It is spiritual milk that causes us to grow up in our salvation (1 Pet 2:2).

How do we get the sustenance of God's life into our lives—our daily bread? The pastoral imagery of Psalm 23 points the way. We allow ourselves to be led into green pastures. God wants to take us to a quiet place beside still waters from which we can drink. Psalm 1 also gives a clue. The person who is blessed by God, like a tree planted by a stream, is nurtured as he continuously meditates on God's Word. Both the sheep in the pasture and the tree by the stream are images of quiet rest in the presence of God—a quiet time.

When we have a quiet time, we feed our souls. We lift our eyes beyond the here and now to the eternal. We lift our hearts from the miasma of mixed motives to the unadulterated Good. We look past the dark god of this age to the God of eternal light. The Lord is present; all creation sings his glory. Through our quiet time, we can know his presence in our work, our family, our recreation—everything.

Guided Quiet Time
The Lord's Attention (Matthew 4:23—5:2)

Yet I am always with you; you hold me by my right hand. You guide me with your counsel, and afterward you will take me into glory. (Ps 73:23-24)

Sunday-morning worship is important to me. I love being surrounded by people who sing hymns in a heartfelt way and pray as if their lives depended on it. But I have found that Sundays are not enough. I need personal time with God as well: just me and God. I need to know that he knows my name and is involved in the details of my life. I need his personal guidance.

Peter, Andrew, James, John and the other disciples must have felt the same need. Jesus often took them aside for personal attention and private instruction. In the Sermon on the Mount we have the most complete and concise summary of Jesus' direct teaching of his disciples. Such personal instruction was not limited to the first disciples. It is available to you and me. All that is required is that we respond, read and listen.

Approach

Someone once commented, "God doesn't have favorites, but he does have intimates." Write a couple of sentences to God telling him that you want to be close to him and know him better.

Study

1. Read Matthew 4:23—5:2. News about Jesus spread throughout Gal-

ilee as he began his ministry. What was Jesus doing and saying to attract such crowds?

2. Consider the large crowd that Matthew mentions. What could be some of their reasons for seeking Jesus?

3. Consider other significant events related to mountains in the Scriptures. Look up the following passages and write out a summary of each one: Exodus 19:20—20:1; 1 Kings 19:11-13; Matthew 17:1-7; Acts 1:10-12.

What might be the significance of Jesus' teaching on a mountain?

4. Why do you think Jesus might focus on his disciples rather than the crowd?

Reflect

1. What would it be like to be following Jesus among the crowds? Write down what you might feel emotionally and physically and what you might hear and say to others.

2. Consider your own motivations regarding Jesus Christ. What would be your reason for being in the crowd?

3. Just as Jesus called the disciples away from the crowd to teach them, Jesus wants to give you the same personal attention. How would you respond if Jesus called you to personally receive his instruction?

4. Write down the hindrances to being a disciple that you find in your heart and turn them over to the Lord.

Pray

Ask God to give you the attitude of a disciple, with a listening ear and a responsive heart.

Pray that Jesus' kingdom would continue to expand and that many would hear his word and receive his healing touch.

[Taken from day 1 of *Sitting at the Feet of Jesus*, by Stephen D. and Jacalyn Eyre, InterVarsity Press, 1993.]

4
Settling in God's Presence

*I*f we want to meet with God, we have to set aside time. This is not easy. Most of us feel that we have too much to do and not enough time. Moreover, our materialistic age teaches us that "time is money." Unplanned time leads to failure, while controlled time, governed by our purposes and priorities, is the key to success.

But as Christians, we find the focus of our culture too narrow, too limited and too secular. For us, the real issue is not "time is money," but *time is holy.* If we let the principles and priorities of material success govern us, we will become spiritually impoverished. We need to order our time for our spiritual health.

God's Time
God built time spent with him into the Ten Commandments. "Re-

member the Sabbath day by keeping it holy" (Ex 20:8). The purpose of this gift of time was to celebrate his creation of the world as well as his redemption of Israel from slavery in Egypt (Deut 5:15).

In the course of a year five feasts were celebrated, two of which lasted a week. These feasts were Passover and the Feast of Unleavened Bread in March/April, Pentecost and the Feast of Weeks in May, the Feast of Tabernacles in September/October, the Feast of Trumpets in late September and the Day of Atonement in early October.

Not only were days and weeks set aside, but years were holy as well. One year in seven, the sabbatical year, was devoted to rest and worship. Two consecutive years, a sabbath year every forty-ninth year followed by the Jubilee year in the fiftieth year, were holy times when all debts were forgiven and all slaves were set free.

What was the message of these feasts? God creates time, meets us in time and orders time. Therefore the use of time is to revolve around him. By observing those designated days, weeks and years, Israel was to experience the centrality of God over and over again. And their celebrations would teach them something essential about God. More than a burden, the days of rest were reminders of God's saving care. They were true holidays (holy days). People were set free from toil and debts to rest, worship and celebrate.

Sadly, Israel missed the significance of this gift of holy time. Because the holy days were ignored, the nation was condemned by the prophets. Through the prophet Jeremiah, God commanded the wayward nation, "Do not bring a load out of your houses or do any work on the Sabbath, but keep the Sabbath day holy, as I commanded your forefathers" (Jer 17:22).

Daniel understood the essential issue. Living in pagan Babylon, he prayed three times a day—morning, noon and evening. He maintained his pattern, even when it got him thrown into the lions' den.

By Jesus' day, the gift of holy time had been turned into a legalistic burden. People couldn't cook or walk over a mile on the sabbath. The sabbath was no longer understood as protected time in which God could be worshiped and enjoyed.

Christians of the Middle Ages ordered time around worship. The day was ordered around the prayer times of Prime, Sext and Vespers. The week was organized around Sunday. The seasons were organized around the Christian festivals of Christmas, Easter, Ascension and Pentecost. And the years were organized around the birth of Christ, B.C. and A.D. Churches kept the time because they had the only mechanical clocks.

Today we have lost the sense that time is ordered by God. Holidays are merely vacation times, and Sundays are days for sports and leisure. Christmas and Easter are times to exchange gifts. Our culture has lost any sense of making time to be with God.

Seizing the Time

How can we establish time patterns that will allow us to meet with God? *We must choose to set aside holy time.* Time focused on God is not just an interruption in our day, but a reminder that all of our time is under his lordship. My father-in-law used to read Scripture and pray at lunch. This gave him half an hour alone with the Lord. A working mother in our church gets up half an hour before other family members, at 5:30 a.m.

Making room for a regularly scheduled time is almost an act of violence initially. I must seize the time and set it aside. Something else will have to give: an hour of sleep, time with friends, a TV program. If this seems like too much of a sacrifice, consider that you find time to eat several meals a day. Shouldn't we be able to find time to feed our souls as well?

We must seek to have regular holy times. They need to be anchored into the routine of our lives. The prophet Daniel used mealtimes of morning, noon and evening. That may not be realistic for you, but you need to find something that is.

Many people prefer early morning. Mark records that at the very beginning of Jesus' ministry, before sunrise, Jesus got up to pray (Mk 1:35). Perhaps lunchtime works better with your schedule, or maybe you can designate time in the evenings to spend with the Lord.

My regular times with the Lord have varied over the years. I like spending time with the Lord at my desk in the morning before anyone else arrives. Then I have a sense of being prepared to face the rest of the day in the presence of God, with the strength and wisdom that he provides.

I go through several stages when I establish a quiet time routine. Initially I have a sense of excitement about doing something new. After a while boredom and resistance set in, and I am tempted to give up. But if I keep going, I come to anticipate meeting with God.

We not only need regular times; we need extended holy times with God that allow for a sense of leisure. In Israel, a whole day, the Sabbath, was given over to rest and worship, as well as entire weeks at the feasts of Unleavened Bread and Pentecost.

Devotional times for most people vary from fifteen to forty-five minutes. This is my normal pattern as well, but I have found that it is not enough to completely satisfy my spiritual hunger. When I take an hour or three or even a whole day to be with God, I sense the depth of his peace, the freshness of his Spirit, the tender affection and quiet of his presence. I find myself longing for and reaching out to God. These longer times make up for the limitations of regular daily meetings, which are limited to Scripture study, a few minutes of quiet seeking and prayer.

How do you set aside extended time? One way is to use the sabbath as it was intended. After church, the Sunday meal and even a look at the paper, there is ample time to be with both the Lord and the family. While I was a theological student, I skipped study on Sundays, even if there was a test on Monday. This gave me time to worship and fellowship without the pressure of getting back to the books. It also reminded me that my grades and learning were gifts given by God, rather than my own achievements.

Initially the practice of meeting with God in holy leisure will seem strange. You may worry about wasting time. Often there is a "restlessness barrier" that I have to break through. But on the other side of the barrier is a rich, full rest.

We need a sense of continuity in our lives to cultivate holy time. Our daily routine needs to be protected. When it is disrupted, setting aside time to be with God is difficult. Students frequently report struggling spiritually during summer vacations and holidays. I find that true for myself as well. In the change of routine, the time and space created to meet with God vanishes. This need to maintain routine in our lives shows the value of the spiritual rule of the monastic orders. Meeting with God flourishes in a sense of rhythm and order.

We need to be flexible in our holy times with God. This may seem to contradict the preceding principle of continuity. But the reality of modern life is constant change. Students' schedules change from term to term and are interrupted by holidays and vacations. Working people are affected by business trips, vacations, changing jobs and deadlines. Families are in constant flux because of the burdens and pleasures of bearing and raising children.

We can cope with changes in our routines if we are determined and convinced in our hearts that meeting with God is important. We can watch for the hour or two, as they come up, to be alone with God. We must not be legalistic and get upset with ourselves when we don't get our usual devotional time. We need to be gracious toward ourselves and determined toward God.

Guided Quiet Time
Settling in God's Presence

My heart is not proud, O LORD,

my eyes are not haughty;
I do not concern myself with great matters
or things too wonderful for me.
But I have stilled and quieted my soul;
like a weaned child with its mother,
like a weaned child is my soul within me
O Israel, put your hope in the LORD
both now and for evermore. (Ps 131)

We are busy people who live in a busy world. But if we are going to spend time with God, we will have to slow down our pace.

We must create a space in our lives to be with God. This isn't so easy. There are always people to phone, letters to write, errands to run. The list of demands on me is endless. But if I am going to meet God, I have to get past these demands to sit worshipfully in his presence. How can I ever control these demands?

First, don't ignore them. It is because they are important to you that they have such power. Richard Foster writes:

> We can give up the need to watch out for number one because we have One who is watching out for us. I sometimes like to picture a box in which I place every worry and every care. When it is full I gift wrap it, placing a lovely big bow on top, and give it as a present to the Father. He receives it, and once he does I know I must not take it back, for to take back a gift once given is most discourteous.[1]

Approach

We must give over our concerns to the Lord. Sometimes I picture myself writing out a list of pressing issues on a "to do" list and then handing it to the Lord.

Study

1. Read Psalm 37:7 and Psalm 46:10. Why is it important to be still?

2. Read Exodus 14:13-18. How was Israel still and active at the same time?

Reflect

1. As you sit before the Lord, give over your responsibilities, concerns and fears. Write down all the things that you have to do. Put the list in a box and make a gift of it to the Lord.

2. How do you feel after turning over your cares to him?

3. What difference will this make in the way you face today?

Pray

Pray through your list. Ask God for wisdom on each item. Ask him to protect you from taking them back.

[Taken from day 3 of *Entering God's Presence*, by Stephen D. Eyre, InterVarsity Press, 1992.]

5

Finding
a Quiet Place

*S*everal years ago I spoke at a conference in a Beverly Hills church. While taking a walk between sessions, I noticed three churches on nicely landscaped grounds in the space of two blocks on one side of Santa Monica Boulevard. On the other side of Santa Monica Boulevard was Rodeo Drive and the business district. This seemed strange to me, and I asked about it.

I was told that the developers who laid out Beverly Hills in the early 1900s didn't want to allot any land to churches because they didn't generate profits or tax revenues. When movie star Will Rogers objected, the developers reconsidered. They squeezed in the churches on a strip of land that had been set aside as a public park. Creating space for God was a grudging afterthought!

Church buildings were once welcome in the heart of business sections. Small towns built in the nineteenth century typically feature a town square with a courthouse. Near the courthouse are often a number of church buildings. The word *city* originally referred to a town in medieval Europe that had a cathedral. Skyscrapers have replaced cathedrals as the heart of the modern city.

Meeting Places in Scripture

Christians in other times built cathedrals not merely for religious extravagance, but because they understood the importance of creating a well-defined, protected place in which to meet with God. We too need structures in our lives that provide a safe, protected place in which we can meet with God. Our busyness in the pursuit of money, recreation and education tends to displace any space for quietness before God.

In the Old Testament when God appeared at a certain place, it was marked as holy—a place set apart for God. Shortly after Abraham entered Canaan, God appeared to him with the promise, "To your offspring I will give this land" (Gen 12:7). In response Abraham built an altar. After Abraham separated from Lot, the Lord appeared again with the promises of countless children and the land to live in. Again Abraham built an altar (Gen 13:18). After Jacob's night of wrestling with the Lord, he built an altar: "How awesome is this place! This is none other than the house of God; this is the gate of heaven" (Gen 28:17).

Holy places were also marked with ebenezers (stone markers) which commemorated God's help. Joshua set up pillars of stones when the Israelites crossed through the Jordan River. The stones were reminders that God had stopped the Jordan. "These stones are to be a memorial to the people of Israel forever" (Josh 4:7).

The ark of the covenant, located in the temple in Jerusalem, presided over the most holy place. When Solomon dedicated the temple, he acknowledged that even the highest heaven could not contain God, much less the temple that he built. Yet, he prayed, "May your eyes be open toward this temple night and day . . . so that you will hear the prayer your servant prays toward this place" (1 Kings 8:27-29).

In John 4:21-24, Jesus affirms Solomon's insight that God is not localized in a specific place. He says that God is not to be limited to a mountain or to Jerusalem. More important than the place of worship is the manner—"in spirit and in truth." Even so, places have their significance in the Gospels. Jesus frequently ministered near the Sea of Galilee and frequently prayed in the desert. His ministry began after forty days in the desert (Lk 4:1-2). He retired into desolate places to pray (Lk 5:16).

The end of history includes a place: the New Jerusalem in the new heaven and earth. A whole chapter in Revelation describes it. In our final state we will not float about disembodied up among the clouds. The holy city is to be a real place: our place and the dwelling of God. In that place our fears, hurts, needs and desires will be satisfied. In the center of the city will be the throne of God, not a skyscraper or cathedral.

Meeting Places in Christian History

The priorities of earlier eras are reflected in the church buildings and cathedrals that dominate town and country. The major tourist attraction in any major European city is a massive cathedral.

Until we lived in England, cathedrals were something I had only read about in history books. I found myself deeply affected by my initial visits to cathedrals. I was overwhelmed by the size of the buildings and the beauty of the artwork. I also felt a striking sense of history—worship had taken place here for eight hundred years or more. And finally, there was a sense of holiness. God was honored in these places. These were places set aside to God. They were holy.

In earlier times, monastic houses were set up to allow entire communities to pursue God. St. Benedict established the first enduring religious community in the sixth century. Over the centuries the Benedictines, Augustinians, Franciscans and other orders provided a focused and ordered environment in which God could be sought.

Finding Meeting Places

We can worship God anywhere, but the pursuit of God benefits from a sense of place. C. S. Lewis once observed that God always seemed less real to him in a motel room. My own experience confirms Lewis's strange observation. A familiar place creates a context for spiritual focus. When we change the place of quiet time, there is a period of transition before we can settle into the familiarity of being with God.

The spiritual and the physical are interconnected in ways that we may not completely understand. When we meet with God regularly in one place, the physical surroundings take on a special significance. The surroundings become friends that invite us into the presence of God and remind us that he has met with us there before. They also foster a sense of anticipation that our holy encounters will continue.

A Holy Seat. My places of study and reflection have varied over the years. Whether I am in my office, a small room in the back of a church, a cubicle in a local retreat center or a booth in a restaurant, I need a table on which I can spread out my journal. There have been periods when my favorite place was a corner booth in the local McDonald's. Some of my best insights about God, life, writing and myself occurred to me there. Wherever we sit down with the Lord, it is important only that it be a place where we can relax and spend leisurely time.

A Holy Path. When I was a new believer, I considered evening walks by the Gulf of Mexico to be holy. Walking along the shore with the wind, waves and sand put me into a seeking mood. When I moved to the Midwest, I went through a period of grief and a sense of separation from God. Eventually walks in the woods and streets around my house came to replace my walks along the shore. In England we lived about a mile from the Underground station. My walks to and from the station became great times of prayer. Not far from our current home is a park with a path around a lake. It is a lovely place to walk and pray.

I find that a well-defined prayer list that is fixed in my mind is essential for effective prayer walks. I keep in mind family, friends, ministry issues, political issues and a variety of other things. Frequently I use the Lord's Prayer as a pattern for my prayers on my walks. I take it one phrase at a time. As I pray through it, I spend time in praise toward God and petition for every essential need.

We need *special* places for spiritual nourishment. I use my desk for business, making calls and writing letters. Consequently, I find it difficult there to make the transition to the sense of quiet necessary to seeking the Lord. Sitting in cafés or going on walks breaks the routine and help me physically and mentally to seek the Lord.

Sometimes my desk is the only appropriate place. Then I try to clear it off, stuffing unfinished work in drawers so I won't see it. The clear desk and the open journal and Bible then become the ebenezers that remind me that I am preparing to meet with God.

We also need *protected* places. If we know that interruptions are impending, it is hard to cultivate the focused heart that seeking the Lord requires. If I know that the phone is going to ring, or that someone is going to knock at the door, or the mail is going to arrive, then I find myself waiting on other people or things instead of the Lord. One way to protect my desk is to get to it before the day starts "officially," being there before the mail arrives and the phone rings.

Finally, we need *familiar* places that carry a sense that God has met us there before. As my feet hit the path of my normal prayer walk, I have a sense that my whole body as well as my mind knows that it is time to pray. When I sit down in the chair that I use for meditation and reflection, I find myself being drawn into worship as my heart reaches out to the Lord.

Recently my wife Jackie and I arranged to go out for a Saturday morning of prayer. We arranged care for the boys, reserved a room at church and spent a morning in prayer. The church room was perfect. It was a special place, different from the ordinary routine; it was a protected place without phones or responsibilities; and it was a familiar place because our church is where we have repeatedly experienced times of spiritual enrichment.

Discipline is the operative word. We need patterns of thought and behavior that draw us away from any improper focus so that we can be open to God and his Word. We must give thought to when and where we do actually sit down and spend time with the Lord. Because our culture does not provide any patterns that help us order our time and place with God, we must seek to establish our own.

Guided Quiet Time
The Beginning of the Gospel (Mark 1:1-8)

New things are exciting. "Bigger," "better," "newer" always catch our attention. New cars shine, smell fresh and drive with zip. But new things get old. Today's new clothes will be out of style next year. New cars lose their shine, and upkeep costs increase relentlessly.

But what if there were something new and fresh that never got old? What if the excitement of new ideas and fresh opportunities continued forever? That is what the gospel of Jesus Christ is like. It began two thousand years ago with the ministry of John the Baptist and Jesus. It never gets old because it is about the eternal God who is the source of new life. Jesus' ministry began two thousand years ago, but because he rose from the dead, it will continue forever. This means that you and I can get in on the action. We too can be a part of this world-changing, life-changing good news ministry of Jesus Christ.

Approach

When you enter a movie theater, your sense of enjoyment is enhanced because you are in a dark room with no windows. Outside distractions are cut off. The movie screen is large, and you are surrounded by sound. Similarly, your sense of encounter with the Lord will be enhanced if you put yourself physically and emotionally in a place where you can focus on the Lord. Seek to focus on God. Write down every distraction that comes your way for the next five or ten minutes. After you have written down your distractions, ask him to prepare you and empower you spiritually to enter into the Gospel of Mark. Write out your prayer.

Study

1. Read Mark 1:1-8. In verse 1, Mark writes about the beginning of the gospel. Describe what is going on in these verses, noting such things as the people, places and times mentioned.

2. In Israel sin was atoned through sacrifices offered by the priests at the temple in Jerusalem. Why then were people coming out to John?

3. The term *sin* isn't used much in our culture. What is sin? How does a sense of sinfulness affect people?

4. John is in the desert, calling people to get ready for the Coming One. How would the desert setting help people in Israel get ready to return to God?

Reflect

1. Place yourself in this crowd gathering to hear John's message. What feelings do you have?

2. John called people to turn away from their sins in order to get ready for the coming of the Messiah. What things should you turn away from to grow in the knowledge of Jesus Christ?

3. Some people think verse 1 is the title for the whole book of Mark, not just the opening verses. Read it again and write out what it says in your own words.

4. Because the gospel that began in Mark is still continuing, you and

I can participate in it! Consider how you would like to experience the spiritual truth of these verses in your life.

Pray
Pray through your personal prayer list.

Pray for our world, that the message of Jesus Christ will bring a turning from sinfulness to the forgiveness that he offers.

Pray that the church will continually prepare itself to welcome Jesus.

[Taken from day 1 of *Daring to Follow Jesus*, by Stephen D. and Jacalyn Eyre, InterVarsity Press, 1993.]

6

Getting Alone
with God

If you are like me, getting up in the morning to have a quiet time is difficult. I found it easier to get up for a class when I was in college or, these days, an early-morning breakfast meeting than getting out of bed for a quiet time. We may tell ourselves that we struggle with a consistent morning quiet time because we don't want to get out of bed. However, I believe that the real issue is that we avoid being alone— whether it's morning, afternoon or evening. When I get up for a class or a breakfast meeting, I am spending time with people. When I get up to have a quiet time, I am spending time alone.

For most of us, being alone and loneliness go hand in hand, and loneliness is painful. Psychiatrists and clinical psychologists speak about it as the most frequently expressed complaint. Listening to the radio, I sometimes think that most of the songs could be summarized by the phrase "Please don't leave me alone." Generation X is described as "a generation alone." They have had to face the consequences of baby boomer parents' struggles to stay together in a culture of marital turbulence and two-income consumerism. The experience of growing up for them has brought a sense of growing up alone.

From the root of loneliness comes destructive fruit. On one extreme, there is the loneliness of the addict who seeks to kill the pain with drugs. On the other, there is the loneliness of a TV watcher who stares at a screen and makes no real personal contacts. In at attempt to cope with the pain of loneliness we may work harder, play harder, perhaps drink or take drugs, and rush into relationships that offer the potential of intimacy, but in the end fail to deliver.

Despite what we may think, loneliness and being alone are not synonymous. Loneliness is being alone and experiencing an inner emptiness. The other side of loneliness is solitude. Solitude is being alone with an inner fullness. If we are to have regular quiet times, we must learn to move from loneliness to solitude.

What Is Solitude?

Solitude is being alone on purpose. Loneliness happens to you. A child who can't find friends to play with, a rejected lover, a new person in town—these are lonely situations. In contrast, solitude is something you choose. When I put on my running shoes and head out the door, I am choosing to be alone. I am looking forward to the benefits that come from the exercise and the opportunity to let my mind roam free as I pass by a lake, glimpse the squirrels and duck under tree branches. I am alone, but I am not lonely.

For introverted people the choice for solitude is fairly easy. Their temperament inclines them to get away from people. For extroverts being alone is almost unthinkable, because they draw energy from being with people. Solitude is important for extroverts, but it comes at a greater cost and must be managed in small doses.

Solitude is being alone for personal growth and accomplishment. As a high-school student, I hated to spend time in my room doing homework. My grades suffered. When I got to college, it was study or perish. I found time to get to the library. Alone, away from my friends and other distractions, I actually began to get passable grades and learn a few things.

Those who are successful learn how to be alone. Whether it is an artist with a canvas, an author staring at a page, a teacher making out a lesson plan or a businessperson reviewing accounts, they know that certain things must be done alone. From that time alone a painting can be put on public display, a book may be published that many will read, a teacher can stand in front of a class, or an accounting can be given to the stockholders and the board of directors.

Solitude is being alone for personal renewal and refreshment. Being mildly extroverted, I like being with people. But after a day of counseling and meetings I am exhausted. I need time in the evening alone before I am ready to face another day.

One of the problems with our world is that it is difficult to be alone. We have phones in our cars so that we can talk while we drive. And then there is the radio. When we come home, there is the television. This continual exposure to voices talking or singing at us creates an emotional deficit. In the end we have nothing to give and we seek to take from others who, like us, have little to give.

The soul has power to replenish if given relational space. Going for a walk alone in the woods, taking time by yourself on the back patio in the summer twilight, lying under the stars—these things bring inner renewal. Of course, if we spend time alone while we restlessly wait for others to call or come over, there is no refreshment. We only feel deprived and our energies are further depleted. The benefits come when we choose to be by ourselves.

Solitude is being alone in order to enhance our relationships. Someone has described marriage as two ticks without a dog. Facing each other with a sense of need, marriage partners bring to their marriage a sense of loneliness with the expectation that the other will take it away. We feel this frustration in all of our relationships. The closer the friendship, the greater the expectation and, consequently, the burden. In our loneliness our relationships become greedy and needy, clinging and dependent.

When we are able to choose solitude, something happens to our relationships. Instead of expecting others to give, we have something to give. Our hearts are open to receive however much or little others can give. There is a sense of open freedom and relaxing peace in being together without demands.

Solitude is being alone in order to be with God. Imagine being in a room with a loved one and watching television while other people carry on conversations. If you want to enjoy being together and have a personal conversation of any depth, you have to get up and leave the room. When we choose solitude for quiet time, we are choosing to leave the room to be with our loved One.

When we are alone, we can discern God's presence. Martin Luther wrote, "I do not know it and do not understand it, but sounding from above ringing in my ears I hear what is beyond the thought of Man." As I sit in solitude, I frequently find that inner fullness that wells up from inside and pulls me into a deep sense of communion with God.

In solitude with God, all the other benefits of being alone come together as well. We find a sense of purpose that stimulates our creativity while bringing personal renewal and enhanced relationships. When we add solitude to efforts to set aside a time and place to be with God, we have the necessary framework for a quiet time.

Biblical Basis of Solitude

In both the Old Testament and New Testament, those who grew in the knowledge of God were called to times of solitude. Abraham's experience of solitude began when he was called from his home in the region of Babylon. God says, "Leave your country, your people and your father's household and go to the land I will show you" (Gen 12:1). Although Abraham left with his wife and a few servants, he was going into a life of solitude, choosing to follow God and leaving his home. The night God gave Abraham the covenant promise of a child and countless offspring and the time years later, when Abraham walked up the mount to sacrifice his promised son, these too were experiences of solitude.

Solitude was a constant part of Moses' life. His first encounter with God at the burning bush was one of solitude. He alone saw the bush and heard the voice. When he received the Ten Commandments on Mount Sinai, he spent forty days alone with God. The tent of presence in which he met daily with God was also a place set apart to be alone with God. In the end of his life, he ascended alone to a mountain to get a glimpse of the Promised Land and then to pass on to the other side of death.

How much of David's life was spent in solitude? As a shepherd boy, he learned to trust God as his shepherd while watching the sheep on the fields of Judah. His skill with the sling that would eventually slay Goliath came from this time with no one but the sheep. Later, when he was king, his life continued to demonstrate the fruits of solitude as he wrote psalms of intense feeling and deep thought and faith.

Jesus' ministry began with a call to solitude as the Holy Spirit took him into the wilderness for forty days. He emerged from that time alone with God having faced down Satan, ready to proclaim the kingdom of God. Throughout his ministry he would go off alone to pray. Luke writes that "Jesus often withdrew to lonely places and prayed" (5:16). When he taught the disciples about prayer, he emphasized solitude: "But when you pray, go into your room, close the door and pray to your Father, who is unseen. Then your Father, who sees what is done in secret, will reward you" (Mt 6:6).

Following Jesus, the disciples were led into the experience of solitude. It began for them in a way similar to that of Abraham. They were called from their family fishing business to a life of dependence (Mk 1:17-18).

In the apostle Paul we see even more clearly the way of solitude. He writes that shortly after his conversion, he was led into a period of solitude in Arabia in which he was instructed by the Lord (Gal 1:15-17). On several occasions he was put in prison. Although his isolation was imposed upon him, he turned it from a time of loneliness into a fruitful solitude. In Ephesians he refers to himself as "a prisoner of the Lord," trusting that the Lord himself was working through his jailers. By his exercise of faith Paul escaped being a victim. From those prison experiences he wrote letters that have spiritually nourished millions of Christians for almost two thousand years.

The last book of the Bible, the book of Revelation, was given in solitude. John was confined on the island of Patmos. While he was worshiping the Lord, he heard a voice, saw a vision and was given a glimpse of the end of history.

Choosing to be Alone

Just as we must seize the time in order to have a quiet time, so we must seize ourselves and our relationships if we are to grow in solitude.

First, we must get away from people—at least those who want to talk to us. You may be able to go into a room and close the door at home. Or you may have to get out of the house.

It helps to let family members know that you want some time alone. Initially, this may be greeted with puzzled looks, but most families will adjust. Roommates will as well. One high-school student I know puts a small cross on his door when he doesn't want to be disturbed. His parents know to leave him alone and that he will come out when his quiet time is over. Perhaps if you are a college student your roommates can get the message you want to be alone when you sit on your bed or at your desk with your Bible and journal open.

With some determination and creativity you can find a way. I can be alone nicely in a shopping mall or a coffee shop. No one talks to me, and I can pray or ponder.

We must also get away from entertainment. Our time and space to be alone with God is aggressively consumed by our entertainment devices. We spend time watching or listening when we could be by ourselves. If we merely got up and turned them off, our excuse of too little time to be with God would vanish immediately.

Television also creates difficulties for solitude because, for most of us, it is in a room where the family gathers. It seems almost disloyal to get up and walk out of the room to be alone. Additionally, the TV's sound goes through walls, around corners and up through ceilings.

We have our television in the basement. Even so, at times the sound comes up through the floor. To cope with this I have a set of headphones. Putting them on with music as a nice background creates a solitude for me in the midst of the noise of the household. If you listen to music to be entertained, then headphones may be a distraction. But if you listen to music as an aid to worship, then it can provide a quiet, reflective tone.

We must get away from responsibilities. Parents, children, students, teachers, employees or executives—we all have things to do. At times our responsibilities are burdens that weigh us down. At other times they provide satisfying projects that we look forward to. Either way, when we choose to be alone, we need to set them aside. They can wait. If we allow them to preoccupy us, then we are pulled away from being with God. They become ghosts and noisy companions that distract us from the rest and refreshment of solitude. I find that the way to put them down for awhile is not to deny or suppress them, but to give them over to the Lord.

Keep Trying

My own experience of solitude is varied. I can be quiet and content for a week or so. Sometimes even longer. But then it changes, and I can't let go of the distractions inside of me or ignore the demands surrounding me. Then there are times when being alone with God is threatening and painful. In those times I bring my loneliness to God and try to learn from it.

Solitude is about relationships. It is also a matter of the heart. We learn to be content to be by ourselves in order to be with God. As we grow in the practice of solitude, our quiet times become quiet. There will be a peace inside. If you have the courage to bring your loneliness to God, he will change it for you too.

Guided Quiet Time

Getting Alone with God (Psalm 16:1-11)

My soul thirsts for God, for the living God.

When can I go and meet with God? (Psalm 42:2)

There is something deep within us that longs for God. It is the inner work of God's Spirit that all God's children have. But that inner hunger can grow weak unless it is nourished. Preoccupation with day-to-day living can choke it out. If you are a student, it may be a concern about grades or finding the right partner. If you are earning a living or raising a family, it may be balancing the budget or moving up the corporate ladder. Whatever it is that fills your mind and your activities, you must learn to put it aside from time to time so that you can focus on God.

Approach

Emotionally and mentally step out of all your personal connections, not because they aren't important, but because you want to come back to them strengthened and refreshed from your time alone with God. Make a list of every person you are connected with. Allow yourself plenty of time. After you have written down every name you can think of, give the list over to the keeping of the Lord.

In your mind's eye turn now from them to him.

Study

1. Read Psalm 16:1-11. David begins by asking God to make him safe. In what ways does David acknowledge that God has been answering this prayer?

2. What does it mean to take refuge in God?

3. Read verses 5-6. How do an "assigned" portion and clear boundary lines contribute to a sense of security?

4. How does David's focus in verses 7-8 create a sense of safety?

5. How does David's knowledge of God affect his attitude concerning the end of his life (vv. 9-11)?

Reflect

1. Spend some time picturing God as a strong fortress surrounding you, providing boundary lines of security. As you do this, consider what he is protecting you from and what he is freeing you to do.

2. David has chosen for God and against other gods. What issues, people and/or concerns compete for your attention and allegiance?

3. David has set the Lord before him. Do that now. Spend time directing your thoughts, emotions, desires, activities and plans toward him. After you have done so, write down how this affects you.

4. David refers to eternal pleasures at God's right hand. Although this looks to life on the other side of death, there are certainly many delightful pleasures from God that we taste now. Consider, how do you experience "pleasure in the Lord"?

Pray

Ask God to teach you how to enjoy him more and find pleasure in his presence.

Ask God to guide you in ordering your day so that you can find time on a regular basis to enjoy being with him.

Pray that those you love would find pleasure in the Lord.

7
Following
a Quiet Time
Pattern

*N*ow *that you have created a quiet time and place, what do you* do during your quiet time?

Prayer and Bible study are the mainstays of quiet times. In Bible study we seek to hear what God has to say to us. In prayer we speak back to him. In other words, Bible study and prayer are the essential forms of a good spiritual conversation. But we must be careful, because the mindset of our age predisposes us to turn almost everything into a technique. While we are doing our Bible study we may somehow lose the conversation, the realization that God is speaking to us, and merely take in information. Or we may look up a verse or two that give us a nice thought for the day. We may not use the Bible at all. It is often tempting to do too much too fast and in the wrong way when we approach God, and that's not good. Our approach robs God of his glory and leaves us in spiritual darkness.

To meet with God, we need to slow down inwardly so that we can relax and open our spiritual eyes and ears. Having done that, we can open the Scriptures and feed our souls on God's Word. Like spiritual glasses, Scripture brings our lives into focus so that we can discern the Lord's presence. After we settle into our meeting with God, we are in a position to pray with spiritual power for ourselves and others.

Warming Up and Slowing Down

At the beginning of a quiet time the task is to get quiet. Being quiet is essential to knowing God. David, king of Israel, wrote, "My heart is not proud, O LORD, my eyes are not haughty; I do not concern myself with great matters or things too wonderful for me. But I have stilled and quieted my soul; like a weaned child with its mother, like a weaned child is my soul within me" (Ps 131:1-2).

As we seek to become inwardly still, we may become aware of inner tumult. We must not ignore these interior demands and voices. We treat our hearts like big, old-fashioned closets. For years, we dump, store and suppress there pains and emotions that we want to avoid. As soon as we become quiet, we sense all those emotions and concerns clamoring for attention. They may seem overwhelming.

The first task in getting quiet is to acknowledge these concerns and give them over to the Lord. Sometimes I write out pressing issues on a "to do" list and then hand it to the Lord. Some people find it very difficult to let go of the list. They have become so attached to their pressing concerns that they are threatened to the core when they consider letting them go.

We need to be quiet so that we can listen for God when we meet with him. For a couple of years my sons had small portable radios with headphones that they carried around with them. They would sometimes attempt to carry on a conversation with me while the headphones were on. My voice was competing with some rock group pounding away in their ears. So I set a policy that I wouldn't talk until the headphones came off.

In our culture it is as if we have headphones strapped on at birth. The music of the world is always blaring in our ears. The voice of God's Spirit gets drowned out. If we are going to be able to hear with our souls, then we need to get those headphones off! John White writes:

> Listening to God is not just something for the mystic who lives in the desert or just for those in Bible times. God is always speaking. To hear his voice is not usually a mystical experience. . . .
>
> To hear him involves no exercise in "tuning into the right frequency" so much as a humble recognition that it is his prerogative to speak and our responsibility to respond.[1]

After we have stopped being busy inwardly, after we have stopped telling God how to run our lives—and the world—there is a full quiet that we can enter into. When you reach this stage, you can just sit back and enjoy being with the Lord.

Reading and Study of Scripture

Once you are quiet, you are ready to meet with God in his Word. We can't be casual about Scripture study. Proper understanding of Scripture requires effort, time and skill. We need to soak in each passage: read, study and meditate on it until it becomes a part of us.

Reading

Step one is to read. Pick a book of Scripture and read through it from beginning to end. For most epistles in the New Testament, a complete reading takes less than fifteen minutes. The Gospels, Acts or historical books of the Old Testament take longer. Once you obtain an overview of an entire book, you can reread favorite passages. They will make more sense because you understand the context.

Studying

Step two is to study. I suggest that you read Scripture like a letter that was written several generations ago. If you are going to make sense of such a letter, you need to know something about who wrote it and the person to whom it was written. This requires a bit of investigation. Detective Sherlock Holmes provides a good model. His ability to pick up clues is marvelous. He walks around asking questions and looking at seemingly insignificant details. Then he wanders off to think about it. Finally, of course, he solves the crime.

Holmes's method involves a principle of observation. We must look closely at details in our search for clues to the meaning of a book or letter. After looking up close, we need to stand back and take it all in. Not only do we have to read a passage several times looking for clues, we have to think about it—a lot. Then we can put the pieces together. When we do that, we will see the meaning of the book in a way we didn't before. "Of course, now I see what that means!"

It's wise to keep a reference book handy that provides background information about what you have read. This information will deepen your insight and perhaps correct any erroneous conclusions you may have reached.

Meditating

Step three is to meditate. J. I. Packer describes meditation as "an activity of holy thought, consciously performed in the presence of God, under the eye of God, by the help of God, as a means of communication with God. Its purpose is to clear one's mental and spiritual vision of God and let his truth make its full and proper impact on one's mind and heart."[2]

In contrast to Eastern meditation, which seeks to empty the mind, Christian meditation seeks to focus and fill the mind with the truth of God. While Eastern meditation puts aside reason, Christian meditation develops the skillful use of reason, considering the works of God and seeking to understand what they mean. Christian meditation also includes the emotions. We focus on God and his Word so much that we feel glad about God's truth, humbled by his law, thrilled with his creation. Christian meditation combines reflection with emotion in such a way as to produce poetry such as the psalms.

Psalms is the book of biblical meditation. Psalm 1:2 describes a godly person as one who meditates: "His delight is in the law of the LORD, and on his law he meditates day and night." The psalms are meditations by David and other godly Israelites. Subjects of meditation include the law (Ps 119), God's unfailing love (Ps 48:9) and his works (Ps 77:12).

When I meditate on Scripture, the love of God or the works of God, I put myself in a quiet, secluded place where I can become immersed in the things of God. Right now I am studying and meditating in Colossians. Paul describes the glorious benefits that we have in Jesus Christ, our supreme ascended Lord. In Colossians 3:2 Paul calls us to "set [our] minds on things above, not on earthly things." As I meditate on this, I ponder on what "things above" and "earthly things" mean. I consider what life will be like when Jesus comes back and what values of heaven I should be living by in light of his return. I long to be rescued from my selfishness, sinfulness and the circumstances of life that I struggle with while I am waiting.

One method of meditation is called *lectio divina*, or "divine reading." It means reading Scripture with a heart of devotion in order to be with the Lord. Basil Pennington describes it this way: "It is not a question of reading a paragraph, a page or a chapter. It is, rather, sitting down with a friend, the Lord, and letting him speak to us. We listen. And if what he says in the first word of the sentence strikes us, we stop and let it sink in. We relish it. We respond from our heart. We enjoy it to the full before we move on. There is no hurry. We are sitting with our friend. . . . We let him speak. We really listen."[3]

As you read, you gain a sense of being nourished in your heart. The disciples on the road to Emmaus experienced that on the resurrection day. After listening to Jesus speak they commented, "Were not our hearts burning within us while he talked with us on the road and opened the Scriptures to us?" (Lk 24:32). This experience is wonderful, but it doesn't happen during every quiet time. Sometimes you just gain information. That's OK.

Some people find the use of the imagination helpful in biblical meditation. Once I was having a quiet time with a new friend who was very active in our church. We were studying Psalm 1, which is about the value of meditating on Scripture. Bill pictured himself as a tree growing his roots by a river. He was shocked, however, when his tree fell over and into the river. We discussed what this might mean. It seemed to suggest that he was so busy doing things for the Lord that he had not taken time to become rooted in Scripture.

There is a spiritual exercise for reflection that I use myself and in guiding others. I make three columns on a page and label them "Experiences," "Emotions" and "Perceptions." In the first column, "Experiences," list events, experiences or major issues. These can be things that happened yesterday, last week or in the past year. Your list doesn't have to be in any special order. Nor do you need to write complete sentences. Just use one or two words that remind you of things you recall.

The middle column, "Emotions," contains your emotional responses to each event listed in the first column. In just a word or two write down your emotions as you can recall them (satisfied, disappointed, pleased, upset and so on). It's important that you pay attention to your emotions. They help you discern what is going on in your heart.

The third column, "Perceptions," is to help you ponder what God is doing in your life. Look over what you have written in the first two columns to find ways that God has been working. Do you see any common themes or patterns? Is there an inner conviction that God has been working in you or through you?

Experiences	Emotions	Perceptions

Prayer

Having spent time with God in quiet and in Scripture, you are in a position to pray with spiritual wisdom and power. Biblical prayer comes from hearts that are shaped by the Scriptures and enriched by meditation.

Prayer is very simple but amazingly difficult. It is something a newborn believer in Christ can do from the very first. Yet it requires lifelong effort. The greatest saints struggle with it. How should we approach God? What should we say? How should we say it? What right do we have to ask God for anything? How do we know that he will answer?

Prayer can be thought of broadly as communion with God, and more narrowly as asking God for help. Telling God what you need is simple in concept but not necessarily in practice. When I pray, I admit that I face problems that are beyond me. I need God's help. The prayers of the Bible include many petitions for help—Abraham seeking a son, David crying out for deliverance from his enemies, Nehemiah asking for help in rebuilding Jerusalem.

We are to pray in Jesus' name. Jesus told the disciples, "You may ask me for anything in my name, and I will do it" (Jn 14:14). This means much more than slapping the liturgical formula "In Jesus' name, Amen" onto the end of our prayers. To understand the meaning of this, we need to put Jesus' teaching in context. It was the night before the crucifixion, and the disciples were overwhelmed with the weight of the moment. How could they carry on without Jesus? The answer was prayer. Jesus assured them that they could ask for help to do the work that he gave them. They were to ask in Jesus' name, meaning that they were committed to doing Jesus' work and fulfilling his commission.

When you and I pray in Jesus' name, we join in the mission. We are making a commitment to do what he wants Christians to do until he returns. Before we pray we must ask ourselves, Do our motives align with his kingdom? This way of praying turns us away from self-centeredness. We can ask for our personal needs, but we must remember that the focus of our lives is obedience to the will of our Lord, not personal gratification. "Not my will, but yours be done" (Lk 22:42).

It is helpful to use a list when we pray. "Aim at nothing and you are sure to hit it," the old saying goes. If we don't have a list, our prayers will probably be wandering, unfocused and haphazard. A prayer list can be as sophisticated as index cards with pictures of people you pray for, or it can be jottings on a sheet of paper. The first couple of pages in the front of my journal contain the names of people I am praying for or issues I am concerned about. As my prayers are answered, I put a mark and a date by my request. God answers prayer all the time, but we often miss this because we aren't looking. When you pray daily and keep a list, you will be able to recognize answers when they come.

There are two extremes to avoid in making a list—being too general or too specific. We can take a cue from the Lord's Prayer. Your specific requests need not be detailed. Tell God what you want. Don't say it repeatedly. Don't elaborate. Just tell him. Pray for one entry on your list, then move on to the next. Jesus cautions against praying like the pagans who think they will be heard because of their many words (Mt 6:7-8). God knows what we need before we even ask. Our prayers are to seek his help, not to inform him or manipulate him.

Our need for daily bread may be expressed as balancing our bank account or seeking a raise. Forgiveness of sins may mean seeking forgiveness for harboring anger toward your spouse or friend. Deliverance from temptation may require keeping a chaste attitude toward someone at work or not fudging on the expense account.

Praying also requires persistence. We must pray repeatedly until we sense that God answers our prayer in one way or another. Those who pray must learn to wait—sometimes for months, sometimes for years. I wonder what Zechariah, the father of John the Baptist, felt when the angel showed up in the temple and announced that a prayer of his had been answered. "Your wife Elizabeth will bear you a son" (Lk 1:13). By that time Zechariah and Elizabeth were far beyond childbearing age.

Waiting on the Lord takes us to the heart of prayer. God works according to his time, not our convenience. We are humbled. But God meets our needs as we wait, giving us refreshment for body and soul. Isaiah writes, "Those who hope in the Lord will renew their strength. They will soar on wings like eagles; they will run and not grow weary, they will walk and not be faint" (Is 40:31).

A great spiritual exercise is to restrict your prayers to questions for a week or so. Don't ask God to *do* anything. Just ask him questions. This exercise reminds us that God knows what needs to be done. Our requests can be short and to the point, as Jesus teaches us to pray (Mt 6:5-13).

Putting It All Together

How long does such a quiet time last? As long as an hour or more, or as little as twenty-five minutes. The goal is balance. You probably won't include all four elements every day. You may spend most of your quiet time settling in and reading Scripture on one day and meditating through a passage and praying on the next.

Keep in mind as well that to focus on one element for an extended period is not healthy. It shouldn't be all Bible study or all prayer or all getting settled. Imagine eating only steak for two months—or only fruit. Although your quiet time will occasionally seem like a duty, that should not be the norm. Meeting with God should include expectation, excitement and desire.

Guided Quiet Time
Security in the Lord (Psalm 30:6-12)
Occasionally I experience what I call the "jerked rug" phenomenon. It happens when I am feeling pretty good about myself, a bit too good. When the rug gets pulled and I stumble, I find that I am not quite as clever or as wise as I thought. As I am forced to face my limitations, I experience anew the wonderful grace of a God who is there to give security far beyond my own capacity.

Approach
Ever have a closet so full of clutter that you were afraid to open it? Often our hearts are like closets into which we throw unwanted feelings and unsatisfied desires. We avoid opening the door because everything will come tumbling out. If our hearts are similarly cluttered, the spiritual and emotional dimension of life is lost. Take some time now to open up your heart. Allow things to fall out. Over the course of this study you will be asking God to help you clean them up. Write down what desires, hurts and concerns you may find. After you have done that, sit in quiet anticipation of what God will do.

Study
1. Read Psalm 30:6-12. How do verses 6 and 7 describe David's sense of dependence on God?

2. What reasons does David present to God in favor of his deliverance (vv. 9-10)?

3. Look over the entire psalm. How would you describe David's re-

lationship with God?

Reflect

1. Difficult circumstances can cause us to reflect on the character of God. How have the circumstances of your life affected your relationship with God?

2. David expresses some of the ups and downs of his life. Consider the last six to twelve months of your life and then chart your ups and downs.

3. Meditate through the ups and downs, picturing the Lord with you through each phase. Once you have done that, write down your insights and emotions.

Pray

Ask God to give you the courage to face the unpleasant experiences of life that may be important but unresolved.

Ask God to give the members of your church the courage to face unresolved conflicts.

Ask God to bring the nations to face the unpleasant experiences of life that produce conflict.

[Taken from day 2 of *Waiting on the Lord*, by Stephen D. and Jacalyn Eyre, InterVarsity Press, 1994.]

8

Quiet Time
Companions

*O*ne of the best ways to enhance our spiritual growth is to share our quiet time with at least one friend—a quiet time companion. Spiritual growth requires that we spend time alone. But once we have spent time alone with God, we need to be able to spend time with other believers.

A quiet time companion can enhance our spiritual growth. Sharing our quiet time with a spiritual friend helps us talk about God. In many Christian gatherings God is an assumed presence. We gather in his name. We sing songs *about* him, and we pray *to* him. But when it comes to his work in our lives, we often talk *around* him. However, when we share our quiet times with someone, God is the subject of our conversation.

Sharing our quiet times can enhance spiritual discernment. We may not be aware of God's working in our lives until we talk about it with someone. Verbalizing our frustrations to a friend may help us see our problems as gifts sent to help us face an inner struggle that we had been avoiding.

Sharing our quiet times can protect us from error. We may think God is directing us in some way, but perhaps we are deceiving ourselves. As we share our hesitations and concerns, our friend can help us explore our sense of leading and consider it in the light of God's Word.

Guidelines

How do you find a friend with whom you can share your quiet time? First, look within your church or Christian fellowship for someone who displays a hunger for God. Pay attention to people who show up frequently. Their attendance may be motivated by spiritual interests. You may find someone at work who expresses interest in the spiritual life. Someone who shows his faith in a work environment is probably pursuing God.

Find someone who is on your spiritual level. A quiet time companion should be a spiritual friend. You want to avoid a discipling relationship, because it can inhibit openness and spiritual intimacy as you move into a one up/one down position.

Find someone who is worthy of your trust. You will be sharing some very intimate information about yourself. The first several times you meet together you may want to share in general terms. As trust grows over time, you can open up more of what you are learning about God and what he is doing inside your heart.

What do you do when you meet together? First, it must be clear that everything you say is confidential. You both must agree to say nothing about your meeting without permission, not even as a prayer request to a few "trusted" others.

Second, agree on when, where and how long to meet. You will need at least an hour for both to share. If possible, spend some time in quiet worship and prayer as well. Decide on the number of times you will meet. A period of six weeks is good to begin with. If things don't work out, you can easily terminate the arrangement. If your meetings are mutually beneficial, you can continue for another two or three months and then evaluate again.

Next, you need to establish the purpose of your meetings: to talk about your quiet times. You must avoid distractions, or you will end up talking about everything but God.

There is no best meeting procedure. Experiment to see what works for you. While one person shares, the role of the other is to listen and clarify with an accepting attitude. Never criticize, correct or counsel. The role of the listener is to be gracious, welcoming and affirming. Keep in mind that you are not there to psychologically analyze, counsel or fix each other. Your goal is to talk about what is happening in your quiet times.

The partner who listens must keep two goals in mind. One is to listen and ask questions that will help the speaker discern what the Lord may be doing and saying in his or her life. The other goal is to help the partner respond to God. When my partner asks me how I feel about God's work in my life, any resistance can be exposed. This opens up channels of communication. If I never face my resistance, my quiet time can slip into mere formalities and dry up.

What to Talk About

Sharing quiet time with a friend can yield helpful insights. Questions that we can ask each other include: Are we able to get quiet? How does our quiet feel? Is there a pull toward God or a dull, lifeless silence? Are we able to give our concerns over to God or do we cling to them and allow them to gnaw at us?

As we talk about settling, we may identify a concern that we can't let go. Perhaps a student is anxious about an upcoming test and can't turn it over to the Lord. Or perhaps a mother continually worries about one of her children at school. Perhaps a businessperson can't turn over concerns about year-end profits.

Such struggles may point to areas of life that have not been brought under the lordship of Christ. The student struggling with the test may fear letting down her parents or damaging future career prospects. The mother may wonder if God can be trusted for her child because a friend of hers from childhood once got hurt. The businessperson may be anxious about profits because of overspending on home remodeling. In prayer he needs to face his stewardship of his resources. As these root issues come out, it is possible to pray about them and see specific results.

In sharing what happens during our settling time, we can examine our emotions. There may be a sense of gratitude. This is the work of the spirit that cries "Abba, Father" within us. It indicates spiritual health. Or there may be a sense of deadness. As we talk about this with a friend, we may discover buried anger. Once we have uncovered our anger, we can tell God about it, seek guidance about a proper response and move on. As we bring these areas to the Lord, we give over the pain of the past and thus free ourselves from its control. Between gratitude and deadness is a sense of turbulence. Anxieties and fears experienced in our quiet time mean that our hearts are alive to God, but there are issues to be worked through. Pay attention to this emotional turbulence and ask God to clear it.

As we share our quiet time, we can also explore what is happening in our study and meditation of Scripture. Quiet time companions can ask each other questions that include: What new insight or knowledge did you learn about God? What seemed to strike your heart in a new way? What seemed to apply to your immediate situation? What do you think that God was asking you to do?

Sharing discoveries from Scripture can be especially invigorating for both partners. Shared insights tend to feed on each other. I may experience new insights when I hear my friend share about the benefits of perseverance from Romans 5. My struggles may take on new meaning as I am reminded that God uses such struggles to work patience into my character.

One of the benefits of sharing study and insights is that we can hold each other accountable. If what my friend is saying about a passage does not make sense as I read over it, I must ask for further clarification. If I just can't see the point, then I must say so. Too often we treat Scripture as putty that we shape to mean what we want it to. Spiritual partners can help each other avoid this temptation.

In sharing quiet times I frequently use the exercise of listing experiences, emotions and perceptions (see chapter six, pp. 62-63). In describing to another what has happened for the past week or so and verbalizing how I felt about it, I can frequently begin to discern God's working.

Once I was sharing from my "Perceptions" column about God's working in my life. Nothing was working out to my expectations, and I felt frustrated. As I talked about this with Bob, he wondered if God was asking me to give up a sense of control. As we explored this possibility, it became clear that God was asking me to "let go." But I did not know exactly how I was supposed to let go. As a few months passed, it became clear that some ministry programs in the church needed radical changes. Changing them was hard, but not as hard as it could have been. I had already been warned. I knew that God was involved in shaping the ministry programs for his purposes, and I could let go by allowing them to change.

Finally, quiet time companions can ask each other questions about their prayers: Who do you feel especially called to pray for? Do you sense that God is hearing your prayers? What answers to prayers have you recently received? What do you find difficult to pray about?

As we talk about our prayers with a friend, we can begin to see God's leading in them. Our prayers for others can start out with a general request such as "God, please help Bob in his job," or "Please help Bill deal with the discipline problems at home." As we pray, we may gain insight on how to pray for Bob's work situation or what specifically to ask for Bill as he sets godly limits for his son. Discussing our sense of leading in prayer with another can clarify just how God is leading us.

Talking about our prayers with a friend helps us discern areas of our own prayer life that need more attention. At one point I was struggling with my calling. I had a sense that God was calling me to another ministry. I found it very difficult to pray about what I should do. When I shared this struggle, I discovered some unresolved pain with a couple of colleagues. Before I could pray freely about my future, I had to face these relational issues.

As we share our prayers with a friend, our faith that God answers prayers will grow. Together we will share a sense of mutual mission in seeking God's kingdom and working together to do his will on earth. There is nothing more exciting and fulfilling than this.

Summary: Questions for Discussion

Settling Down and Warming Up	☐ *Are we able to get quiet?*
	☐ *What is the tone or feel of our quiet?*
	☐ *Is there a pull toward God or a dull lifeless silence?*
	☐ *Are we able to give our concerns over to God or do we cling to them and allow them to gnaw at us?*

Reading and Study	☐ *What new information are we learning about God?*
	☐ *What seemed to strike our hearts in a new way?*
	☐ *What seemed to apply to our immediate situation?*
	☐ *What do we think God may be asking us to do?*

Reflection and Meditation	☐ *How do we see God working in our lives?*
	☐ *What may God be saying to us through our experiences?*
	☐ *What may God be asking us to do in and through our circumstances?*

Prayer	☐ *Whom do we feel especially called to pray for?*
	☐ *Do we have a sense that God is hearing our prayers?*
	☐ *What answers to prayers have we recently received?*
	☐ *What do we find difficult to pray about?*
	☐ *Are we able to ask for help?*

Overall Issues	☐ *Do we have a sense of meeting with God?*
	☐ *How are we responding to God?*
	☐ *What might the Lord be saying to us?*

Having a Quiet Time Together

Not only is it helpful to talk about our quiet times, but it can be very helpful to have a quiet time together. Initially it may seem strange, two people sitting in a room being quiet for twenty or thirty minutes. However, it can be extremely powerful. There is something enriching about the shared silence. Many times I find the room is filled with the Lord's presence in a warm, full quiet that is often tender and affectionate. I used to think this was my imagination. But more often than not, my partner shared the same sense of presence.

What do you do in a quiet time together? After a period of quiet that allows you to settle, look at Scripture and pray. Follow the usual procedure. However, because you have been working through your quiet time together, there is a sense of immediacy and freshness about it. You aren't sharing about quiet times over the past week or two, you are sharing about what happened in the past fifteen or twenty minutes.

Sharing a quiet time as well as meeting to talk about our quiet times challenges the secularized mindset that we have inherited from our culture. We have been socialized not to speak about God in public. We tend to carry this mindset into our private lives and our Christian gatherings. However, as we talk about our quiet times, we learn to recognize God's presence. We open up our spiritual ears and reverse the process of God-blindness. We begin to repair the rods and cones of our spiritual eyes. God becomes more than someone we know *about.* We know *him* from our personal experience and experiences with friends. As we have quiet times in which we meet with God, not only do we learn to be with God but we learn to see and hear him in all his world.

Guided Quiet Time
We Are Chosen (Ephesians 1:1-6)

In a seminar on prayer I asked participants to chart their lives on a large sheet of paper. The charts were to illustrate the role of prayer in their lives.

During the sharing time, a couple of themes emerged. First, prayer was more prevalent in the ups and the downs of life than in the plateaus. Second, in the hard times prayer grew from a response to God. It wasn't so much that people prayed and God answered, as that God began to help and then we asked for it.

Does that seem strange to you? It was to me, until I thought about it in the light of the Scriptures. As with all religions, Christianity shares a belief in a divine being who should be worshiped. In other religions, the divine being is pursued for favors. In contrast, Ephesians teaches us that God's nature is to seek us out first.

Approach

We all have needs. These needs can hinder us from knowing God, or they can help us know him better. A first step in spiritual growth is understanding our needs. The next step is knowing how to give them to God so that he can help us. Begin your approach to God today by asking him to bring your needs to mind. As you write them down, ask God to share the burdens with you.

Study

1. Read Ephesians 1:1-6. Paul refers to Jesus Christ in each of the three lines of his greeting (vv. 1-2). Read over these verses several times. What can you discern about the apostle Paul, the Ephesians and God from his greeting?

2. God the Father is the subject of praise in verses 3-6. Reread these verses several times as well. How would you describe Paul's attitude towards God?

3. Paul's enthusiasm is a result of what God has done for us in Jesus Christ. According to verses 3-5, what specific results come into the life of a Christian because we are chosen and loved by God?

4. Explain the role of the Father and the role of Jesus Christ in bringing us these benefits.

Reflect

1. In verse 3 Paul writes that "we have every spiritual blessing in the heavenly realms." Imagine that you have made it safely to heaven. How do you think it will feel?

In Christ you are assured of that eternal safety. What difference does this knowledge make in the way you live?

2. The first spiritual blessing Paul mentions is that we are chosen by God. Think about a time when you were chosen for a task or given a special honor. How did it affect you?

How much greater is the privilege of being chosen by God! Picture yourself in a crowd at a beach. As you are standing there, Jesus comes along and invites you to follow him. How do you respond? What anticipations and reservations do you experience?

Pray

Thank God for the spiritual blessings that he has given you.

Ask God to give you the same attitude of gratitude that is reflected in the apostle Paul.

[Taken from day 1 of *Enjoying Christ's Blessings*, by Stephen D. and Jacalyn Eyre, InterVarsity Press, 1994.]

9

Quiet Time Dynamics

I once went eight months without a quiet time. It was not a good time in my life, but it was a spiritually powerful time. During this period, I was spiritually nurtured by worship services and Christian friends. I struggled with feelings of guilt but just couldn't bring myself around.

For several months before this dry spell I had set aside several hours a day to seek the Lord. Repeatedly, I had called out to him to change me. When he began to answer my prayers, it was not what I was expecting. Not only my quiet times but all of my life was shaken and transformed by God's work. It was a confusing period, and I coped by avoiding quiet times altogether. God didn't reject me during that time. When I was able to begin again, he was there with a warm welcome.

Quiet times go through phases. Sometimes they are rich and sweet, other times dry and boring. This diversity of experience no longer surprises me. My quiet times vary widely because the work of God's Spirit in my life varies widely. I used to feel guilty about these ebbs and flows. I don't anymore. Knowing God is an ever-changing experience.

Using Your Emotions

When we sit down to be with God in our quiet times, our emotions are involved. God is a person, and a relationship with God, just like any other personal relationship, involves emotions. With my emotions I sense his affection for me, embrace his Word and react to his commands.

I realize that mentioning emotions invites controversy. Talking about emotions among Christians can be, well, emotional. Some pride themselves on their emotional restraint. Let me say that I am not advocating great outward displays of emotion. Others take pride in their ability to display emotion. They should keep in mind that emotions are natural responses that vary from time to time and should not be forced or manipulated.

Scripture tells of godly people whose emotions were central to their encounters with God. David experienced tremendous heights and depths in the course of his life, as described in the Psalms. Elijah, Jeremiah, Jonah and Habakkuk, to mention a few, experienced their own ups and downs.

Are emotions useful indicators of our spiritual life? Could our down times signal spiritual need rather than mere depression? Jonathan Edwards used the term "religious affections" to describe our emotional response to God. He too valued emotions as means of spiritual insight. Edwards wrote of "a sense of heart wherein the mind not only speculates and beholds, but relishes and feels."[1]

When critics dismissed the First Great Awakening in New England as merely excessive emotion, Edwards defended it by saying that God was not interested in mildly affected worshipers. God desires those whose hearts burn with a desire for him. Edwards also pointed out that spiritual affections are not merely emotional highs. True spiritual affection is manifested in our love for God. Are we growing in appreciation of God's might, majesty and beauty?

When I was a new believer, I experienced great swings in emotion. I was told that these would level out as I approached spiritual maturity. But though I was a Christian leader in college, then spent four years at seminary and a good number of years in ministry, my swings didn't level out. If anything, my feelings became more intense. But as time went on, they became less unsettling; I stopped fearing that God had left me. Eventually I learned that because my relationship with God is a personal encounter, I must give myself permission to feel both the ups and the downs.

Quiet Time Phases

I have discerned five different phases in my quiet times: occasional quiet time, determined quiet time, study quiet time, desert quiet time and devotional quiet time. Each phase has its own characteristics, its own strengths and weaknesses, its own dangers and delights. The first two, occasional and determined quiet times, deal with frequency—*how often* we have a quiet time. The study quiet time focuses on *what we do* in a quiet time. The last two phases, desert and devotional quiet times, are distinguished by *how we feel* during a quiet time.

We should not expect to move through the phases in a particular order. I will discuss each phase in terms of Scripture, prayer, our emotions, frequency, our sense of the Lord's presence and our reasons for practicing quiet time as a spiritual discipline.

Occasional Quiet Time

The occasional quiet time is not disciplined. Scripture reading tends to be the "skip and dip" method. I pick up the Bible whenever I feel the need and read wherever it falls open. (My tendency is to end up in the Psalms when I slip into this phase.) This quiet time is like eating on tne run; I grab a sandwich, an apple or a candy bar as I rush through tne kitchen and out the back door.

Prayer in the occasional phase tends to be haphazard and task-oriented. I pray only when there is a need: "Lord, help me with this" or "Lord, please do that." Even when I do sit down to be with the Lord, there is little sense of worship. I am usually so busy inside that I can't hear (much less join) the Spirit as he cries "Abba, Father" within me.

Emotionally, my response to the Lord is on again/off again. Sometimes I am excited about him; other times I am not. Most of the time, things other than God are on my mind and heart.

Most of us go through the occasional phase, but it is not a good place to remain. God is moved to the edge of our lives. Spending time with him is not a priority. There is always one more phone call to make, one more page to read or one more urgent meeting to attend.

Determined Quiet Time
A determined quiet time is the opposite of the occasional quiet time. It is practiced every day without fail. Whereas the occasional quiet time comes and goes depending on our feelings, we practice the determined quiet time regardless of our feelings. Time is set aside each day, and nothing is allowed to get in the way.

A formal reading plan, possibly reading through the Bible in a year, replaces the "skip and dip" method. (I have found the *One Year Bible* a great help.) Or you may use a devotional guide that picks up a thought from selected Scripture texts and then tells a related story with a moral.

Like Scripture reading, prayer in the determined phase tends to follow a predetermined pattern on a daily basis. One friend has a set of prayer cards with people's pictures stapled to them and concerns listed beside the pictures. He prays through them each day. My practice is not so elaborate. I have a list on a piece of notebook paper that I keep current, scratching through names or issues as the prayers are answered while adding new names to the bottom of the list. The advantage of having a daily, set pattern is that certain people and issues receive the benefit of our consistent prayers.

The determined quiet time is a necessary phase of our spiritual walk. We need to meet with the Lord in a disciplined way to counter the influence of our modern world as well as our natural spiritual resistance. Some of us are more disciplined than others. The determined quiet time is important for me because I am not naturally disciplined. As I set aside time to be with the Lord, read Scripture and go through a set pattern of prayer, I am spiritually strengthened.

While a daily quiet time has great benefits, it can also become a snare. We may worry about skipping a day because we fear that God will be displeased with us. Or we can slip into a self-satisfied attitude about doing our daily religious duty. It is easy to place a check on the calendar, thinking, *So much for God today; now on with other things.*

If your determined quiet time has become a mere habit, it might be good to skip a few quiet times. A couple of years ago, my prayer partner mentioned that his quiet times were drying up. At one point in our discussion I made a shocking suggestion: "Stop praying so much." I knew he was seeking the Lord and could handle my seemingly heretical suggestion. I was not surprised when a month or so later he reported a freshness in his times with the Lord.

Study Quiet Time

The key distinctive of a study quiet time is the serious study of Scripture. If a half-hour is set aside for a quiet time, at least twenty minutes of it is Scripture study. An in-depth study of a passage using commentaries and a Bible dictionary is not unusual.

The study quiet time sinks our roots deep in Scripture. We lay up a rich store of spiritual truth that we can draw on throughout our lives. As we see how God works in the pages of Scripture, we learn to recognize his hand in our own lives. As we see how people responded to God, we are inspired—perhaps to seek God as David did, or to be more obedient than Saul was.

All that time in study leaves less time for prayer. Leisurely devotional worship gets crowded out. Prayer time is cramped: short, intense and task-oriented. It easily turns into a shopping list of things for God to do and problems for him to solve.

In a study quiet time, it is possible to learn all kinds of information about God but not encounter God. Our study of Scripture may become a purely mental experience. We tend to assume that because we are studying Scripture, we are in touch with God. Remember the issue for our quiet time: "Am I meeting with God?"

Desert Quiet Time

Good quiet times promote spiritual growth. Surprisingly, this deeper growth can lead to unexpected dryness. When we move into a desert quiet time, there is a temptation to think that we have done something wrong. The desert quiet time is not a pleasant experience. It's like living alone in a desert. There is a sense of empty loneliness. Our quiet times seem to dry up. If we feel anything at all, it is a sense of desolation. God seems absent.

A longing for God accompanied by an aching sense of his absence is common in Scripture. The psalmist writes in Psalm 42, "My tears have been my food day and night, while men say to me all day long, 'Where is your God?' " (Ps 42:3). David cries out, "O God, you are my God, earnestly I seek you; my soul thirsts for you, my body longs for you, in a dry and weary land where there is no water" (Ps 63:1). In another place he cries, "I am worn out calling for help; my throat is parched. My eyes fail, looking for my God" (Ps 69:3).

Nothing seems right in our quiet time or any other area of life. Reading or study of Scripture has a sawdust-dry quality. The pleasure in study that we have known before is gone. Now the words on the page are nothing more than words.

Prayer is also flat. Our prayers for others seem to rise no higher than the ceiling. Worship and adoration seem mere formalities; songs that we might sing are heavy and laborious.

Emotionally, there seems to be nothing inside except an aching sense of emptiness. All religious affections seem gone.

Because a desert quiet time requires great effort, I find that it is practiced irregularly. (My eight-month lapse of quiet time referred to at the beginning of this chapter was due to a desert period.) There is a gnawing need to meet with God along with a frustration in his absence. This desire and frustration lead to an on-again/off-again cycle. It seems to make no difference whether we have a quiet time or not. If we don't have a quiet time, God seems absent. If we do have a quiet time, God still seems absent.

Outwardly the desert quiet time and the occasional quiet time look similar. Both are erratic and inconsistent. But the two are different in nature. The occasional quiet time is erratic because God is not a priority. The desert quiet time is erratic because of an aching thirst for God that we can't seem to satisfy.

Maintaining a regular meeting with the Lord is important during this time, despite the difficulty. When this phase is over, we will discover wonderful benefits. Many things that I know and teach about the Lord have come from desert times.

David was blessed by God in the desert. He spent ten years in the desert running from Saul after God had promised him the throne. During this period David learned to trust God for his promises. He also developed political skills as he led the outcasts and soldiers who came to his side in the desert.

This desert time can last a week or a year. When I was in seminary, I went through a period of four years during which God seemed absent. I believe that God wanted my theological learning to be more than an academic experience. In the midst of this time I began to understand why St. John of the Cross called it "the dark night of the soul." Don't be discouraged if it lasts a long time; others have endured even longer times of dryness. Modern believers, surrounded by physical abundance and recreational distractions, need the ministry of the desert.

The temptation of a desert experience is to conclude that there is something wrong with us; perhaps we have sinned or are drifting away from the Lord. (Sin and apathy do separate us from the Lord, but that is not what I am writing about.) Or perhaps we need to read more Scripture, or pray longer, or pray differently.

We become overwhelmed with a sense of God's holiness and our sinfulness. This experience feels like a purifying fire. The aching dryness of the desert continues until a work of the Spirit is completed in our hearts, and we are moved into the pleasure of God's presence.

We should not be in a hurry to get out of a desert time. God will lead us out when he is ready. Richard Foster writes, "Be grateful that God is lovingly drawing you away from every distraction so that you can see him. Rather than chafing and fighting, become still and wait."[2]

Devotional Quiet Time

Spending time with God is more than a duty or a struggle; it is a great pleasure. In the devotional quiet time we enter into this pleasure in a special way. In the beginning of his *Confessions*, Augustine writes, "You stimulate [us] to take pleasure in praising you, because you have made us for yourself, and our hearts are restless until they can find peace in you."[3] In a devotional quiet time we are invited by God to enter and enjoy this satisfying rest.

I turn to Scripture passages that I have already studied in some depth.

I spend time chewing over a passage until, with Paul in Ephesians, I marvel at the spiritual blessings that have been given to us through Jesus. Or I experience with Peter the unspeakable joy of receiving the goal of my faith, the salvation of my soul.

Sometimes it is helpful to use your imagination to enter into the passage—feeling, smelling and hearing what is happening. I know that many people are not comfortable with using the imagination in this way. If so, ignore the next paragraph. I use this sort of approach because Scripture is full of images. I believe that I am honoring the Lord's intent when I take them so seriously that I give all my senses to understand and experience them.

Psalm 23 is a favorite of mine. I imagine myself in a restful green pasture. The sun is shining warmly on me, and the blue sky has a few drifting white clouds. A couple of large trees provide just the right shade. I find myself alone with the Lord, away from the pressures that burden me. As I settle, I find a living faith inside me that the Lord is indeed present. Along with David, I know the reality of the Lord who is restoring my soul.

Prayer in the devotional quiet time is woven into meditation on the Scriptures. It is rich and varied with fewer lists. Less than half of my prayer time is taken up with petitions and intercession during such devotional times.

Words are not always necessary in this devotional time. I have been delighted to read of Joyce Huggett's experience in *The Joy of Listening to God.* "What I heard in those times of listening was more than a voice. It was a presence. Yes. I heard the Lord call my name. But I also 'heard' his tenderness. I soaked up his love. . . . I had never delighted in God in this way before. And it had never occurred to me that God wanted me to linger in his presence so that he could show me that he delighted in me."[4]

The devotional quiet time is filled with emotion. A hunger for the

Lord exists along with a sense of being filled. You may feel a pulling on your heart that draws you to the Lord, a calling out that increases at his touch. Often there is a sense of warmth, love and joy. Anger, even fear may be present. Always there is a strong sense of God's presence. You know that he is with you.

The devotional quiet time generally lasts longer than other types and requires some leisure. Five minutes fade into fifteen and then an hour. This sense of unhurried leisure may be uncomfortable as you first enter into a devotional quiet time. You wonder if you are merely wasting time and should be doing something more productive. If these thoughts occur, stop to remind yourself of the eternal value of being with God.

Our busy lifestyles don't lend themselves to the leisure that a devotional quiet time requires. The devotional quiet time is practiced on a regular basis—perhaps not every day, but several times during the week. You may take an hour or two one day and then only brief times for the next couple of days.

While the devotional quiet time is most delightful, I have discovered that I don't stay there. Sometimes God gives us that delightful and deep sense of worship; sometimes he doesn't. God doesn't show up on cue, nor does he come to us in ways that we demand. The enduring reality of such pleasure in worship won't come until we see the Lord in heaven.

Temperament

Our temperaments have a great deal to do with what happens in our quiet times. People who are methodical and detail-oriented may gravitate toward the determined quiet time that focuses rigorously on doing one's spiritual duty. Those who tend to be spontaneous may skip the determined phase altogether, perhaps settling in a study quiet time for a while and then slipping back into an occasional quiet time.

I have a spontaneous temperament. I don't like to settle into one way of doing things for very long. I have a natural inclination to avoid set routines. Sometimes I find it necessary to be very determined on a daily basis. At other times, I make it a goal to have four or five quiet times during the week and feel good about it if I have three or four.

Whatever our quiet time experience, there is no place for self-condemnation or pride. When we do well, it is surely a gift of his grace to us. When we do poorly, being either irregular or legalistic, we shouldn't be surprised. God isn't. The goal in having a quiet time is to live in the presence of God, not to rack up impressive spiritual achievements.

Conclusion

Spiritual growth is a combination of God's initiative and our response. We can choose to ignore the voice of the Spirit. We can banish God to the edges of our busy lives, to the borders of consciousness. We can limit our practice to the occasional quiet time, thinking of God now and then and rattling off prayers in a haphazard way. Our spiritual lives will remain shallow.

Or we can respond to his inner workings and be drawn to him. As God works, we will sense a pull and call inviting us deeper. As the psalmist wrote in Psalm 42, "Deep calls to deep in the roar of your waterfalls" (Ps 42:7). As we sense this pull, it is up to us to follow.

Guided Quiet Time
Listening to God

This is my Son, whom I love. Listen to him! (Mk 9:7)

I have other sheep that are not of this sheep pen. . . . They too will listen to my voice. (Jn 10:16)

If we want a personal encounter with God, we must not only stop being so busy but also stop talking so much at God when we pray. Prayer easily becomes a monologue: "God, please do this, please take care of that." A monologue is boring to the person who is forced to listen and exhausting to the person who has to keep up the unceasing flow of words.

Today you are going to take a different approach. Resist telling God to do anything. Spend your quiet time asking God questions and then sit in expectation to hear what he will say.

> Speak, Lord, for I, Your servant am ready to hear You.... The children of Israel said to Moses: Speak to us and we will hear you, but let the Lord not speak to us, lest perhaps we die for dread. Not so, Lord, not so, I beseech You. Rather I ask humbly with Samuel the prophet that you speak to me Yourself.[5]

Approach
Turn your "to do" list over to the Lord. Write down how you feel after you have done it.

Study
1. Read Habakkuk 2:1-3. What does Habakkuk say to God and how does God respond?

2. Read Psalm 32:8. Ponder God's promise of instruction. Do you expect him to instruct you?

Reflect
1. To help you listen, make a list of questions and concerns you would like God to address.

2. Ask God what he thinks about your problem with _____. Ask God what he wants you to do about _____.

Sit back and wait quietly to see what God will say.

Does it seem strange to actually listen for God to talk back? John Powell writes:

> The Lord . . . puts his ideas into my mind and especially his perspectives. He widens my vision, helps me to see what is really important in life, and to distinguish the really important from the unimportant. . . . He comes to me in the listening, receptive moments

of prayer, and he transfuses his power into me.[6]
What did you learn from this experience?

Pray
Tell God that you want to grow in the ability to discern his voice. Pray the prayer of Thomas à Kempis at the beginning of this study.

[Taken from day 4 of *Entering God's Presence*, by Stephen D. Eyre, InterVarsity Press, 1992.]

10
Quiet Time
Tools

*Y*esterday I noticed several loose doorknobs in our house. I am not particularly handy, but I do have several screwdrivers and a small can of oil. In no time the doorknobs were fixed. In the same way, a few tools can keep our quiet time in good working order. We don't need to be very "spiritually handy" or have a large library of biblical and theological wisdom. If the doors to our quiet times aren't swinging open smoothly or there seems to be a catch in the latch, we can bring out a few spiritual tools to tighten things up and smooth out the catches.

Fasting, journaling and Christian literature are tools that I have found especially helpful. Used wisely, these can bring depth, variety and inspiration into our lives. Fasting puts us in touch with our spiritual and physical appetites; keeping a journal sharpens our spiritual senses; reading Christian literature puts us in touch with like-minded companions who are experienced and articulate about meeting with God.

Fasting

Fasting is a spiritual discipline that is broader than our quiet times. We may set aside half an hour for a quiet time, but a fast goes through a day or more. It is a helpful tool, however, because as a spiritual discipline, fasting enhances our spiritual sensitivity. It is partially or completely abstaining from food for the purpose of seeking God. Fasting plays a significant role in the Scriptures. It was used as an emergency measure when things looked desperate. David fasted when he sought God for the life of his dying child (2 Sam 12:16-23). When Judah was invaded by an overwhelming army, king Jehoshaphat called a national fast (2 Chron 20:3). And when the Jews of Persia were to be massacred, Mordecai and Esther called a fast to seek God for deliverance (Esther 4:16).

Sometimes fasting expressed repentance, as when the exiled Jewish nation returned to the Promised Land under Ezra and Nehemiah (Neh 9:1). As Ezra read the Law, the exiles discovered how far they had departed from the ways of God. Fasting was their repentant response.

Fasting was also used as a means of dedication and preparation. Jesus fasted for forty days in the wilderness prior to the beginning of his ministry (Mt 4:2). Paul and Barnabas fasted prior to their missionary journeys (Acts 13:1-3).

Fasting is one of the last spiritual disciplines I explored. I like to eat, and so I avoided it. But while meditating on Jesus' teaching about fasting in the Sermon on the Mount (Mt 6:16-18), I realized that it *was* for me.

As I began to fast, I saw that food is promoted endlessly. "Eat, eat, eat" is the insistent, incessant message. It tests my resolve to place God above my appetites each time I fast. Like no other discipline, fasting involves all of me, body and soul, in the pursuit of God. When my body is hungry, my appetite working overtime and my will wavering, I am reminded that I have chosen God above all other desires. Hunger actually becomes my friend. Every hunger pang I feel reminds me to lift my requests to God. Each food commercial is an opportunity to say no to food and yes to God.

I fast periodically, usually during times of special need. A couple of times I fasted when I needed God's direction in my ministry and career. Once I fasted in regard to a fundraising deficit. There are times when I feel out of touch with God, ministry and family. Fasting in these situations lifts my spirit and strengthens my faith. For the past several years I have chosen to fast for Lent. Fasting at this time helps me enter into the pain of Christ's work on the cross.

How do you actually go about fasting? On a twenty-four hour fast I eat nothing after the evening meal until the time of the evening meal on the following day. Actually that is only missing breakfast and lunch. A thirty-six hour fast means I eat nothing after the evening meal and skip all meals the following day. It's also possible to do a selective fast, abstaining from certain types of food. You might skip meat for a period of time, or coffee or soft drinks. I find this type of fast harder than total abstinence.

Extended fasts require some thought. If you go longer than thirty-six hours, it's wise to fast selectively. Nutritionists tell me that eliminating the amino acids that we get from protein for more than a day can alter our body chemistry and have negative effects on the heart. Going on an extended fast for me usually means restricting my intake to raw fruits and vegetables, with some milk or cheese for protein.

Fasting differs from dieting. There is a power to abstain from food on a fast that isn't present in a diet. Once while finishing an extended fast, I was called on to work in the kitchen at a conference I was attending. Surprisingly, the temptation to eat was negligible, and I experienced an unaccustomed joy in serving others. If I had been dieting, I would not have responded with such goodwill or restraint.

Shortly after Jackie and I were married, we met an elderly neighbor named Mrs. Bibbs. She invited us to visit her later in the evening for what Jackie and I assumed would be dessert and coffee. However, that was not what Mrs. Bibbs served. It was clear that she had been cooking and baking all day, maybe for several days, and it was spread out grandly on the table for us to enjoy. But we had eaten a full meal just before we came. All that great food, prepared with much thoughtfulness, was not in the least appetizing.

Of course we ate, profusely thanking our hostess for the wonderful meal. After each serving, she insisted that we have another serving and then another. Not wanting to disappoint her, we ate and ate. By the time we got up from the table, I was in considerable pain.

In the world we are surrounded by people who are saying, "Have some more, have some more, have some more." However, when we fast we are saying, "No, thank you. I'm saving room in my life for Someone else."

Journaling

Reading and writing have always played an important role in the Christian faith. From Moses' account of the Exodus, to the disciples' record of Jesus ministry, to the apostle John's vision of the new heaven and earth, God's people have been directed by the Spirit to write down their experiences with him. Although we aren't writing inspired Scripture when we journal, we do enter into an experience of God through the written word.

When we journal, we write down what we think, feel and learn as we meet with God. We describe on paper what is going on inside our hearts. We can also record our prayers and our questions for God. This enhances our spiritual discernment of God's presence and work in our lives.

You may find it hard to express thoughts on paper initially. I have found that writing in a journal functions as a siphon. As I write down a word or two, new words and insights come. Suddenly doors open, the logjam breaks and the words begin to flow.

Writing in a journal helps me to pray. Sometimes I have a sense of communication with God just by going over my concerns mentally, saying my prayers in my heart. But sometimes I seem to be talking only to myself. My remedy for that is to write out my prayers. Once I write down what I want to say to God, I usually sense that a real dialogue is taking place.

Develop your own style of journaling. When I write out my prayers, I seldom use complete sentences. A word or a phrase on the page is usually enough to bring before the Lord. I also write down my questions for God. "God, what do you want me to do about _____?" Or, "God, what are you going to do about _____?"

Writing down general thoughts and ideas that come to mind during my quiet time has proven useful. This can stimulate insights that answer questions from previous days. However, these insights often raise other questions. So I write them out in the form of prayer.

One day I was reading through several months' worth of journal entries. It became clear that I was reading a conversation, a dialogue between two people. Someone was asking questions, and someone else was answering! It dawned on me that I couldn't claim credit for my brilliant insights. God had been answering my questions all along.

A couple of months ago I struggled with anger. A thoughtless word from a close friend set off a powder keg inside me. I tried to give my anger over the Lord and let it go, but I couldn't. So I went off to a back booth at a local McDonald's and began to write. Surprisingly, my anger came out as poetry. Expressing my feeling on paper enabled me to identify the roots of my anger. I also found the Lord waiting for me in the depths of the pain. As I let the anger go, it let go of me. I became free to respond to the situation reasonably rather than emotionally.

Try recording your reflections at the end of your quiet time. You will deepen your spiritual insights as you reflect back on your interaction with God. We "re-cognize"—think again—about our time with him. This will reward us with new insights into the ways that God is working within us.

Practical Details

Keeping a journal notebook to review in later years can be helpful because it provides a written record of your pilgrimage with God. On the other hand, throwing away your notes at the end of your quiet time can be very freeing. Your interaction with God is the important thing, not the writing itself. Once you have expressed yourself to God on paper, your purpose has been served.

If you do keep your journal sheets, be sure to include the date and place of each entry. We have done a fair amount of moving, and it is interesting to look back on thoughts recorded in Atlanta, Jackson, Nashville or London.

Don't be legalistic about keeping a journal. If you want to keep it daily, that's great. But writing in it a couple of times a week or a couple of times a month is great too. Both offer opportunities to reflect and record the work of God in your heart.

Christian Literature

Christians throughout the ages have written about their thoughts and experiences with God. Their writings can enrich our quiet times. Some books were written to be used as devotionals—aids to worship. The most famous is probably *The Imitation of Christ.* It was written just before the Reformation by Thomas à Kempis. Protestants as well as Catholics have used it ever since. For each day there is a bite-sized thought filled with practical spiritual wisdom. Passing references to purgatory and a fourth section of meditations on the Lord's Supper (the Mass) have been omitted from most Protestant versions. The fact that Puritans, Pietists and Protestants of every generation have found this book worth "sanitizing" is a testimony to its continuing value.

A popular devotional guide of the twentieth century is *My Utmost for His Highest* by Oswald Chambers. I know people who work through it and then begin all over again. And there are any number of devotional magazines. I especially like the material produced by Scripture Union. It seeks to be contemporary, biblical and practical.

The danger of using a devotional guide is treating it like spiritual fast food. We read the bite-sized thought, glance at the Scripture reference and then we are off to take on the day. What happened to meeting with God?

The benefit of using a guide is that we share another Christian's insight and experience with God. This can enhance our own personal spiritual encounter with God.

Some books teach us how to cultivate a devotional life. The earliest devotional manual ever written was the *Conferences of Cassian*. In the fifth century Cassian traveled around the Egyptian desert and Palestine interviewing monks. He put together a record of those conversations and in so doing created a model for all spiritual instruction manuals to follow.

Since Cassian, thousands of instructional manuals have been written. Twentieth-century authors whose instructional books have helped me tap into the wisdom of early spiritual guides are A. W. Tozer, Richard Foster, Henri Nouwen, Joyce Huggett and Eugene Peterson. Reading these and other instructional works can enhance a quiet time, not just because they give information on how to have a quiet time but also because they impart a spirit of devotion. In reading about how to pray, we are drawn to God in a way that inspires and encourages prayer.

Some books not written as devotionals can be aids to worship. Right now I am reading a book by a contemporary theologian that many would find dry and boring. It's not to me. I feel the pull of God as I read it. In the morning, with a cup of coffee and my journal, I read a couple of pages on my back porch. As I read, I am inspired to think about God, to appreciate God and to grow in my thought life about God. Every few sentences I stop to savor a thought in the freshness of the morning. My own thoughts of God are stretched as I appreciate a brother in Christ who loves God.

Don't pass up classic works that have been studied through the ages: *The Confessions of St. Augustine*, *The Institutes of the Christian Religion* by John Calvin, *The Works of Luther*, *The Journals of Wesley* and *Religious Affections* by Jonathan Edwards, to mention a few. These people and others like them had great thoughts about great experiences with God. When we read them, we are taken deeper into the knowledge of God than we could ever go on our own. Standing on their shoulders gives us a better glimpse of heaven than we get standing on our own two feet.

Guided Quiet Time
The Revelation of Jesus Christ (Revelation 1:1-3)
Frankly, I'm surprised at the widespread positive attitude toward the Bible. A large number of people still believe that the Bible is more than a merely human book. Even those who are not regular churchgoers or diligent Bible students believe that there is something special about it.

Graham, a friend of ours in England, would gather a crowd by pointing to a piece of cloth he dropped on the sidewalk and shouting, "It's alive!" When people came running to see what he was pointing to, he would lift up the cloth to reveal a Bible. Taking up the Bible and waving it in the air above his head, he would begin to preach to his listeners about the virtues of the Bible.

The Bible is alive. Something happens when you read it. Something reaches up from the page to address the mind and the heart. Something (Someone) challenges, provokes, stimulates and entices. This effect was experienced by the two disciples on the road to Emmaus after they met the Lord: "Were not our hearts burning within us while he talked with us on the road and opened the Scriptures to us?" (Lk 24:32).

Approach

In Revelation 1:3, a blessing is offered to those who read, hear and take to heart the book of Revelation. Read it silently and then out loud. Determine to think about it during your day. Read it out loud now and write a prayer asking the Lord to allow you to take it to heart.

Study

1. Read Revelation 1:1-3. What various means of communication are used in the verses?

2. Who are the people involved in sending and receiving the revelation?

3. What assurance are we given that the messages about the future are trustworthy?

4. The revelation is about "what must soon take place." There are different interpretations of this. Some think it refers to the first century, while others think it refers to what will happen throughout the unfolding history of the church. Still others hold that it refers to what will happen at the end of time, and a few include all of the preceding. What do you think?

Reflect

1. The word *revelation* means "uncovering." The book of Revelation is about the revealing of Jesus Christ. Imagine that there is a veil on your heart. Ask the Lord to remove it so that you may see his presence in your life. Sit for a while and allow him to work. Write down your impressions and emotions.

2. The time frame of Revelation is the impending future. Jesus wants us to know what is going to happen. How would your behavior be

affected if you knew what Jesus was going to do in your life within the next week? Consider your work, your family, your friends, your time and your money.

Pray

Ask the Lord to come back soon.

Ask the Lord to give a sense of anticipation for his return.

Pray for several fellow believers, that they would grow in a love for God's Word.

[Taken from day 1 of *Anticipating Christ's Return*, by Stephen D. and Jacalyn Eyre, InterVarsity Press, 1994.]

11

Quiet Time Discipleship

*D*ave *greeted me in the hall one Wednesday night and asked if* I had a few minutes to talk. After a full evening of teaching, I thought about asking him to call me in the morning. But there are times when schedules must be changed. I sensed that this was one of them. His casual manner was masking anxiety.

It had recently dawned on Dave that throughout his life he had been experiencing his relationship with God through other people. He had always hoped that knowing God through others would be enough. And in the past it had been.

Now all that was changing. God was calling Dave to know him face to face. I knew it was my role to open up a spiritual door. So we spent some quiet time together. Dave gave over his wife, daughter, work, church activities and business to the Lord. Dave's secondhand experience became a personal embrace of love between God and his son. If I had merely given Dave a pep talk on Christian commitment and sent him on his way, I don't think that the meeting or the divine surrender would have taken place. But in the quiet, he was able to make a life-changing personal commitment.

Quiet Times for Discipleship

A couple of years into student ministry, it dawned on me that my focus was off. Working with college students, I taught Bible study skills, evangelism, leadership development, small group dynamics and apologetics. But something was wrong. God was an assumed presence, not the focus of ministry.

I wondered if quiet times might address my concern with focus. So I invited a student named Ned to meet me in the student union. We both had our Bibles and notepads. Before we began, we agreed not to talk until our half hour was over. We read Scripture, prayed and then cultivated an attitude of listening silence. In the beginning I considered it my responsibility to make this quiet time work. I was the discipler, and Ned was the disciple. Shortly into the quiet time, however, I realized that Jesus was the discipler, not I.

After that experience with Ned, I began to invite several students each semester to have quiet times with me. Most of these were spiritually powerful experiences. But some quiet time discipling produced a negative reaction. I learned that I needed to identify and invite those who were hungry for a personal encounter with the Lord.

When we use quiet times as a discipling tool, we function as a spiritual guide while those to whom we minister grow in discernment. For a semester, the student leadership team at a university in the South met weekly to share a group quiet time. They called themselves a "listening team." Each quiet time session was opened with the question, "Lord, how do you want us to serve you?" Over the course of the semester, members of the group sensed that they were being led to evangelism.

As the "leader" in the group, I was not the source of vision. Members of the group "heard" from the Lord, not me. On the other hand, I was more than an appendage. My role was to begin by calling us to the Lord, and in our discussions afterward to help us measure our perceptions against the background of Scripture and sound doctrine. The Christian leader facilitates discerning what the Lord is doing so that the group can respond and follow him.

Our church's monthly leadership meetings occasionally use a brief quiet time. When our direction is not clear or when there is sharp disagreement, we may spend time in silence. During this quiet time, we give over our concerns to the Lord and seek to listen for his direction. Afterward, we debrief. This discernment process has gotten us through impasses and a few tense conflicts.

Using quiet time as a discipling tool rescues us from an unhealthy dependence on technique and methods. Ours is a technique-oriented culture, and it is natural for us to adopt a technique approach to ministry. However, quiet time takes the focus off technique. The Lord is the one we expect to direct us and bless our efforts. When we base our ministry in quiet time, the issue becomes not *how* to do it, but *Who* is doing it.

Using quiet time as a discipling tool rescues spiritually hungry hearts from false activism. Occasionally someone comes to me with a desire to do more for the Lord. But doing things for God is not an acceptable substitute for cultivating a personal relationship with him. I suggest that the most important thing to do for the Lord is get to know him better through quiet time. The individual who is established in meeting with God is in a position to do ministry.

Quiet times can open doors to evangelism. In response to the inevitable question, "How do I know that there really is a God?" my response is, "Ask him; he'll tell you himself." I instruct potential converts to set aside some time to explore the possibility of knowing God. They begin by just speaking into the air and asking God to make himself known. Then I tell them to read one of the Gospels and keep a journal of their thoughts about God for a week or two. Finally they are to keep their eyes open for "God-incidents," those "coincidental" circumstances that let us know that someone is working in the events of our lives.

Among those who accept my challenge, the conversion rate is high. In a follow-up meeting I find that most have already given their lives to the Lord or are looking forward to praying a prayer of commitment with me. Those who come into the Christian faith in this way know for certain that Jesus is here and that he can communicate with them. Since they began their spiritual life through a meeting with God, the continuation of a regular quiet time is entirely natural.

Means

Encouraging people to spend time with God is one of the most strategic things we can do. What would the church of Jesus Christ be like if a majority of Christians had quiet times each week? How can we go about cultivating a quiet time ministry?

It is important to encourage quiet times by sharing a quiet time. Beginners may read the Bible and pray without any expectation of a personal encounter with God. They may not be able to settle inwardly enough to cultivate the sense of quiet so necessary for a quiet time. When they are guided by someone who is familiar with quiet time, they acquire a taste for it.

For most people, an early-morning quiet time is best. Many people can only meet before work. Will, Carl, Todd and I met together for a year each Friday morning from 6:00 to 7:00 in a lounge at church. We finished by 7:00 so that they were able to get to work on time. Their Friday quiet times spilled over to the rest of the week. Todd started having quiet times with his wife. Carl started getting to work early and shutting the door for half an hour for his quiet time.

Discipling by means of a quiet time is an exciting, revolutionary action. Moses asked Pharaoh to let Israel go into the desert for three days to worship God. Pharaoh was not amused, and the battle began. By means of a quiet time we follow Moses, inviting people to come out from the world to meet God in the desert.

In quiet times as a means of discipleship we invite God back into the center of our lives. As we practice quiet time we come to know him as the One who is here, Immanuel—God with us.

Guided Quiet Time
The Final Meal with Christ (John 13:1-5)
As you read these verses, you are entering into a sacred experience. You will be standing on holy ground. Jesus is going to die, and he is spending his last moments with those who have been most dear to him on earth. Every word that comes out of his mouth during this final conversation will be remembered, thought about and meditated upon by those who hear them. Every action will be relived in the minds of those who have loved and followed him.

Often, people who know that they are dying withdraw into themselves. Their pain, loss, grief and fear are all-consuming. But Jesus continued to love. He wanted his followers to know that they were loved, and he demonstrated this love freely in word and action.

As one who loves Jesus, enter into this holy moment. Look. Listen. Feel. Prepare yourself to experience in a new way "the full extent of his love."

Approach
Jesus wants you to know his love. What words or ideas come to mind when you think of the love of God?

How would you evaluate your sense of the Lord's love? Consider whether you need to understand and know God's love more in your head or in your heart—or both.

Study

1. After reading John 13:1-5 for background, focus on verse 1. What does Jesus know, and what light does it cast on the impending events?

2. The impending events take place against the background of the Passover. Look up the following verses in Exodus and summarize them in your own words: Exodus 12:12-13, 21-23, 29-30.

3. How do these verses from Exodus help you understand what Jesus was facing?

4. As he writes about upcoming events, John does not mention that Jesus is about to be crucified. Why not?

Reflect

1. What might Jesus feel as he faces his disciples and the future?

2. We have all said goodby to loved ones. Recall some of your most difficult goodbys. Write down the names of those you were separated from and some of the thoughts and feelings you experienced.

3. Imagine that you are about to finish your time in this world and return to your heavenly Father. What concerns do you have?

Pray

Pray that God would give you a spirit of wisdom and revelation so that you might know him better.

Ask God to bless your friendship with fellow Christians, that you might grow in love for each other.

[Taken from day 1 of *Abiding in Christ's Love*, by Stephen D. and Jacalyn Eyre, InterVarsity Press, 1994.]

12

Becoming a
Quiet Person

I *wear several hats. I am a father, a husband, a pastor, a friend, a* brother and a son. On some days, I change hats easily.

Today I don't feel like I have done a very good job of balancing the roles of pastor and father. As my two older boys move through high school, I struggle to give them what they need from a father. I am away from them more than I should be. On the other hand, there is more to do at the church than can possibly be done. I'm grateful for two other pastors and several lay leaders who share ministry responsibilities with me. Still, there are tasks that are not being covered.

When I feel pressured by competing responsibilities, I have a choice. I can stress out, or I can pray. Today, I chose to pray. Praying through the activities and agendas of the past week, I began to see the ways in which God is active and present. I felt my spirit lift as God met me, shaped me and challenged me to new growth. After my quiet time, I didn't feel any more competent, but I knew that my responsibilities weren't mine alone. A quiet peace filled the place where there had been anxiety.

Spending time with God makes a difference in our lives, right down to the depths of our character. You could say that spending time in quiet time makes one into a quiet person.

Don't misunderstand what I mean by a quiet person. I'm not talking about a passive, shrinking-violet sort of person who sits in a corner and seldom speaks. Nor do I mean someone who never gets excited, upset or angry. On the contrary, a quiet person is active and productive. A quiet person feels anger, indignation, frustration, fear, desire and more. But a quiet person experiences these emotions in the context of time alone with God, which produces a Spirit-directed maturity.

The Biblical Picture of a Quiet Person

Abraham, Moses, David and Jesus were quiet people. But only Jesus was quiet from the start. The others became quiet as they grew in the knowledge of God.

Abraham became a quiet person. As he walked with God, he moved from the cowardice of twice denying that Sarah was his wife to the courage of offering Isaac as a sacrifice. His walk to the mount of sacrifice was characterized by a quiet, determined obedience. When Isaac inquired about the sacrifice, Abraham replied, "God himself will supply it."

Moses moved from a rage that murdered an Egyptian slave driver to the disciplined heart of a real leader. His anger led him to smash the tablets of the Law and later lash out at the rock when the people failed to trust God. But he grew. We can detect a quiet tone in Psalm 90, which he wrote toward the end of his life: "Teach us to number our days aright, that we may gain a heart of wisdom" (Ps 90:12).

David too was a quiet person. As he fought giants, led armies, united his country and established a dynasty, he found time to write psalms of reflective worship. In David we see a quiet heart. On the one hand he can write, "The LORD is my shepherd, I shall not be in want" (Ps 23:1). He can also write, "My life is consumed by anguish and my years by groaning; my strength fails because of my affliction, and my bones grow weak" (Ps 31:10).

Jesus epitomized a quiet person. Confronting hostile adversaries, demanding the submission of shouting demons, sleeping in the midst of a storm while the disciples panicked, imploring God in Gethsemane or shouting out on the cross, he lived from a "gentle and humble . . . heart" (Mt 11:29). Isaiah writes of the coming Messiah, "He will not shout or cry out, or raise his voice in the streets. A bruised reed he will not break, and a smoldering wick he will not snuff out" (Is 42:2-3). It is from this place of quiet that Jesus invites us to find rest for our souls (Mt 11:29).

When we live from the quiet, we don't need masks, façades or appearances. The quiet people of Scripture had a settledness, an authenticity, an integration of the inward and the outward. They were not hypocrites, showing one face to the world while hiding another face with a different disposition.

Being a quiet person is a disposition of character. There is no need to be in control or controlling. Nor is there a need to be manipulative, competitive or demanding. A quiet person can be firm, express disappointment, ask for what he or she wants and advocate what is important. This freedom comes from the experience of quiet time with God. As we spend time with him, our souls and the cells of our bodies come to know that Jesus is Lord and that he is working in our circumstances, whatever they be, for his glory and our good.

As we learn to be quiet people, we find that though we are more integrated between the inner and outer aspects of our person, we still live on two levels. On one level we can be coping with day-to-day experiences—driving a car, talking to a friend, working at a desk. On another level we can have an underlying sense of the presence of God. Somewhere deep inside we know that God is with us—indeed *within* us. We sense that he is supporting us even while we know that we are submitted to his authority and are living in obedient response to him.

Learning to be quiet doesn't mean that our lives will be easy. Every quiet person in Scripture lived in the midst of turbulence and struggle, and you will too. You may have to face the unexpected sickness and death of someone you love. Career obstacles may stand in the way of cherished hopes and dreams. Your hopes for a happy home and a "perfect" marriage may collide with the reality of past pains and patterns of behavior that produce more frustration than affection. What will make the difference will be the way you choose to face these battles. The issue is spending enough time with God so that the quiet works its way inside.

As we spend time quietly with God, a change comes inside us. We find a willing submission to God and satisfaction in his presence. Along with rest and refreshment we receive a sense of our Shepherd's guidance, direction, protection and provision.

Once we have experienced that inner quiet, even in the midst of "the valley of the shadow of death" we can have a settled courage. This experience of quiet is more than cognitive. It is a way of being. The quiet moves from outside us to inside us, invading us as we are immersed in it. I believe this is what Paul had in mind when he wrote, "Do not be anxious about anything, but in everything, by prayer and petition, with thanksgiving, present your requests to God. And the peace of God, which transcends all understanding, will guard your hearts and your minds in Christ Jesus" (Phil 4:6-7).

Keeping at It

If you are spending some time in quiet each day, but the Lord seems absent, you may need to extend your time with God to forty-five minutes or more, and occasionally even longer.

I sponsor three-hour retreats of silence at our church on occasional Sunday afternoons. Only a few brave souls showed up at the first one. But almost all who attended felt that even three hours wasn't long enough! Many since have reported discovering a different quality to their time with God, a more tangible sense of his "being there."

If we are to become spiritually healthy people, we may have to change our spiritual chemistry, just as it is sometimes necessary to change our physical chemistry. In a period of about four years I gained forty pounds. When I finally improved my diet, the results weren't so great: I didn't lose any weight! Then I began walking two miles a day. A few pounds came off, and I stabilized at thirty-five pounds above my desired weight.

I began walking four miles a day. Still nothing, except that I could eat normally without putting on weight. Then I began to run three miles a day. After two months of this, still nothing! Middle age was taking its toll. My weight began to drop only when I adopted a routine of running over three miles. I had to increase my metabolic rate for over forty-five minutes a day as well as cut down on my fat intake before my system would begin to alter the way it processed food. As my system changed, my cardiovascular system improved. The outward effects began to show in reduced inches around my waist.

I believe that there is a direct parallel between my weight loss experience and our quiet times. Getting in shape spiritually will probably require just as much exertion. We must keep at it. If we spend time with God, eventually the spiritual conditioning of our hearts will show itself in ways that we and others will be able to see.

Relax and Be Quiet
As you seek to become a quiet person, be gentle and gracious with

yourself. Don't push too hard or be too demanding. I remember teaching my sons how to swim. Before the lessons could begin, they had to get used to the water. Once they relaxed, they began to enjoy the water. Only then did I begin the lessons.

You too need to relax. Your heavenly Father is with you in the water of life. Instead of clinging to him in a state of panic, let go and trust him to lead you in your spiritual lessons. As he spoke through the psalmist thousands of years ago, he still speaks: *"Be still, and know that I am God"* (Ps 46:10).

Guided Quiet Time
Learning to Be a Quiet Person (Psalm 23)

Drawing on the book *Moby Dick* by Herman Melville, Eugene Peterson calls our attention to the power and effectiveness of a quiet person.

"There is a turbulent scene in which a whaleboat scuds across a frothing ocean in pursuit of a great, white whale, Moby Dick. The sailors are laboring fiercely, every muscle taut, all attention and energy concentrated on the task. . . . In this boat, however, there is one man who does nothing. He doesn't hold an oar; he doesn't perspire; he doesn't shout. He is languid in the crash and cursing. This man is the harpooner, quiet, poised and waiting. And then this sentence: 'To insure the greatest efficiency in the dart, the harpooners of this world must start to their feet out of idleness, and not out of toil.' "[1]

Being quiet does not mean we aren't doing anything. Nor does being quiet mean that we aren't being effective and productive. The harpooner had to be rested and quiet so that he would be ready to act at the right time. Through Isaiah God says, "In repentance and rest is your salvation, in quietness and trust is your strength" (Is 30:15).

Psalm 23 uses pastoral images to convey the effects of being quiet. If we spend time in the "green pastures" and in "the house of the Lord," we will find that we can rise to the challenge of life—be it be a white whale in the sea or a nameless, faceless enemy in some dark valley of the shadow of death.

Approach

Write out Psalm 23, copying it word for word. As you write it out, personalize it so you know that it applies to you.

Study

1. David declares that God is his shepherd. In what specific ways is David experiencing this?

2. In what ways does David respond to God's caring presence?

3. What is the meaning of the phrase "I shall not be in want"?

4. David portrays God's presence in three contrasting situations, "green pastures" (v. 2), the "valley of the shadow of death" (v. 4) and a battlefield (v. 5). How does God meet David's need in each situation?

5. David writes that he "will dwell in the house of the Lord forever" (v. 6). Considering that the temple had not yet been built, what do you think he means?

Reflect

1. I summarize each verse in my own words as follows:

Verse 1: Submission and Satisfaction

Verse 2: Rest and Refreshment

Verse 3: Guidance and Direction

Verse 4: Confidence and Comfort

Verse 5: Protection and Provision

Verse 6: Presence and Peace

Try using your own words. Or, if you like mine, personalize the phrases. For instance, for verse one you might write, "I choose to submit to the Lord as my shepherd and be satisfied in the ways that he leads me."

2. Imagine that you are in a place of green grass, blue sky and quiet

water. Sit there until you find the quiet working its way inside you. Write down how it affects you and how it affects your sense of God's presence.

3. God is a shepherd who guides us. When we are quiet, we can discern his leading and respond to it. Think back through the past week. How has the Lord been guiding you?

4. David says that God makes him lie down in green pastures. How has God put you in a situation where you had to slow down?

How did you respond?

Pray

Pray that your church will find ways to create green pastures, places where people can spend time being quiet with the Lord.

Ask God to make you a quiet person who lives in response to his shepherding.

Notes

Chapter One: The Benefits of a Quiet Time
[1]J. I. Packer, *Knowing God* (Downers Grove, Ill.: InterVarsity Press, 1973), p. 19.

Chapter Two: Why You Need a Quiet Time
[1]Stephen Eyre, *Defeating the Dragons of the World* (Downers Grove, Ill.: InterVarsity Press, 1987), p. 127.

Chapter Three: What Is a Quiet Time?
[1]A. W. Tozer, *The Pursuit of God* (Old Tappan, N.J.: Revell, 1987), p. 16.
[2]Jonathan Edwards, *Religious Affections* (Edinburgh: Banner of Truth, 1986), p. 305.
[3]Gerald May, *Addiction and Grace* (San Francisco: Harper San Francisco, 1988), p. 1.

Chapter Five: Finding a Quiet Place
[1]Richard Foster, *Meditative Prayer* (Downers Grove, Ill.: InterVarsity Press, 1985), p. 15.

Chapter Seven: Following a Quiet Time Pattern

[1]John White, *Daring to Draw Near* (Downers Grove, Ill.: InterVarsity Press, 1977), p. 14.

[2]J. I. Packer, *Knowing God* (Downers Grove, Ill.: InterVarsity Press, 1973), p. 56.

[3]M. Basil Pennington, *Centering Prayer* (New York: Doubleday, 1982), p. 193.

Chapter Nine: Quiet Time Dynamics

[1]Jonathan Edwards, *Religious Affections* (Edinburgh: Banner of Truth, 1986), p. 198.

[2]Richard Foster, *Celebration of Discipline* (New York: Harper & Row, 1978), p. 91.

[3]St. Augustine, *The Confessions of St. Augustine,* book 1.1.

[4]Joyce Huggett, *The Joy of Listening to God* (Downers Grove, Ill.: InterVarsity Press, 1986), pp. 33-34.

[5]Thomas à Kempis, *The Imitation of Christ* (New York: Doubleday, 1989), p. 104.

[6]John Powell, *He Touched Me* (Allen, Tex.: Argus, 1974), p. 70.

Chapter Twelve: Becoming a Quiet Person

[1]Eugene Peterson, *The Contemplative Pastor* (Dallas: Word, 1989), p. 33.

Spiritual Encounter Guides *from InterVarsity Press*
by Stephen D. Eyre & Jacalyn Eyre

If you've enjoyed the quiet times in this book and would like to try some more, look for Spiritual Encounter Guides. Each of these provide a month of devotional exercises and Bible study questions to help you find intimacy with God. The workbook format provides space to record your thoughts and ideas.

Abiding in Christ's Love. Discover how to live in the personal presence of Jesus Christ through John 13—17. In this record of Jesus' most intimate conversations with his closest followers during his last days on earth we discover how his Spirit will care for and work through us, as he worked through the disciples.

Anticipating Christ's Return. These quiet times in Revelation show us who Christ wants us to be and what he wants his church to be like as we await his return. Find hope for today as you get ready for the future.

Daring to Follow Jesus. Following Jesus means opposition. But there is also a crown for those who persevere in this challenge. These studies will point you to the promise that sustains us—one day we will reign in heaven with Jesus.

Enjoying Christ's Blessings. Discover the multitude of spiritual blessings Christ offers us through these quiet times in Ephesians. We are chosen and redeemed.

We have a Lord who hears our prayers. The church provides caring and nurture. And families and friends stand with us against evil.

Entering God's Presence. An introduction to the basic components of the Christian life—spending time with God in prayer, study and meditation.

Sinking Your Roots in Christ. Sometimes being a Christian is tough. There are difficult choices to make. Maturity comes slowly. These quiet times in Colossians show us how to find grounding in Christ.

Sitting at the Feet of Jesus. In the Sermon on the Mount we can experience Jesus' personal teaching. He shows us the way to live, offering comfort, encouragement and challenge.

Waiting on the Lord. If you wonder what God has planned for you and why he takes so long, this guide will offer you comfort through the Psalms. It will show you how to put your faith in God when patience and hope feel impossible. Most of all, it will help you to seek God's direction and assurance.